Advance Praise for Leave YOUR Legacy . . .

"I firmly believe that we get ahead in life through our choices. Being great is just that—a choice. *Leave YOUR Legacy* is a resource that illustrates the process that will lead you on the path to greatness. Read it, and learn to release your potential."

—**Aeneas Williams,** NFL Hall of Fame cornerback, fourteen-year NFL veteran, and eight-time Pro-Bowler

"As you read Ben Newman's book, I know you will be more inspired than ever to leave a powerful legacy. Ben and I share many similarities on our paths of life, and we connect deeply on this concept of legacy. We both know that life is temporary, but the legacy you leave is eternal. For this reason I'm excited that Ben has delivered a life-changing message in the form of a story that will drive you to think differently about your life and embrace the story of the legacy you are writing. The title to this powerful story so appropriately reminds us, leave YOUR legacy."

—**Jon Gordon,** *Wall Street Journal* bestselling author of *The Energy Bus*

"Ben's passion is to fire up everyone he meets. His energy is contagious. *Leave YOUR Legacy* will challenge you to uncover your drive, passion, and potential. Thank you, Ben, for showing me how to make a difference."

—**Teri Griege,** inspirational speaker and author, cancer survivor, and Ironman triathlete

"True fulfillment in life is about embracing the journey. I tell my players everyday: 'Don't dwell on the past—learn from it, and compete to be the very best YOU can be each day.' That is what allows you to succeed in the future. Your destination doesn't define you; your journey does. This is what I love about *Leave YOUR Legacy*—it embodies these truths."

—**John Papuchis,** defensive coordinator, Nebraska Cornhusker Football

"*Own YOUR Success* connects you to your life's purpose. *Leave YOUR Legacy* will redefine your thinking to embrace change and leave an impact on others."

—**Will Compton**, NFL linebacker, the Washington Redskins

"Ben Newman is one of the most inspiring and passionate people I have met. *Leave YOUR Legacy* is a true testament to Ben's desire to impact the human spirit."

—**Jason Selk**, director of sport psychology for the 2006 and 2011
   World Champion St. Louis Cardinals

"Ben Newman is a master at bringing out the best in people, as you will soon discover as you read a story that gives you the tools to help you reveal and write our own legacy."

—**Shep Hyken**, business expert and *New York Times* bestselling author of
   The Amazement Revolution

"Ben has once again nailed fundamental principles for living a truly exceptional life. His legacy will be in interrupting the thought patterns of thousands (or maybe millions) and inspiring them to remove self-imposed limitations and achieve more than they ever dreamed they could."

—**Andy Parham**, CEO, DATU Health

"*Leave YOUR Legacy* is a home run. Ben Newman uses a fascinating parable to teach profound lessons on how a person can take life to the next level. If you want to live a happier and more meaningful life, read this book."

—**Adam Loewy**, top U.S. trial attorney, the Loewy Law Firm

LEAVE
YOUR
LEGACY

Foreword by Jon Gordon,
Wall Street Journal *bestselling author of* The Energy Bus

LEAVE
YOUR
LEGACY

THE **POWER** TO **UNLEASH YOUR** GREATNESS

BEN NEWMAN

Author of the National Bestseller Own YOUR Success

GREENLEAF
BOOK GROUP PRESS

Published by Greenleaf Book Group Press
Austin, Texas
www.greenleafbookgroup.com

Distributed by Greenleaf Book Group

For ordering information or special discounts for bulk purchases, please contact Greenleaf Book Group at PO Box 91869, Austin, TX 78709, 512.891.6100.

Design and composition by Greenleaf Book Group
Cover design by Greenleaf Book Group
Cover images:
©iStockphoto.com/MoreISO
©iStockphoto.com/malerapaso

Cataloging-in-Publication data is available.

ISBN 13: 978-1-62634-167-8

Part of the Tree Neutral® program, which offsets the number of trees consumed in the production and printing of this book by taking proactive steps, such as planting trees in direct proportion to the number of trees used: www.treeneutral.com

TreeNeutral®

Printed in the United States of America on acid-free paper

15 16 17 18 19 20   10 9 8 7 6 5 4 3 2 1

First Edition

Dedicated to my children, J. Isaac and
Kennedy Rose. My mother, your grandmother,
taught me the profound lesson of LEGACY.
It is now our responsibility to show you how to
fight for yours each and every day.

In loving memory of
Janet Fishman Newman

*When you are inspired by some great purpose,
some extraordinary project, all your thoughts break
their bonds: Your mind transcends limitations, your
consciousness expands in every direction, and you
find yourself in a new, great, and wonderful world.
Dormant forces, faculties, and talents become alive,
and you discover yourself to be a greater person by
far than you ever dreamed yourself to be.*

—Patanjali

CONTENTS

Foreword

Every one of us is going to leave a legacy. It just depends on what kind. So what kind of legacy do you want to leave? I encourage you to think about it, because knowing how you want to be remembered helps you decide how to live and work today. If you are not sure what kind of legacy you want to leave, here are a few types to consider:

> **A Legacy of Excellence**—Saint Francis of Assisi said, "It's no use walking anywhere to preach unless your preaching is your walking." To leave a legacy of excellence, strive to be your best every day. As you strive for excellence, you inspire excellence in others. You serve as a role model for your children, your friends, and your colleagues. One person in pursuit of excellence raises the standards and behaviors of everyone around them. Your life is your greatest legacy, and since you only have one life to give, give all you can.

A Legacy of Encouragement—You have a choice. You can lift others up or bring them down. Twenty years from now, when people think of you, what do you want them to remember? The way you encouraged them or discouraged them? I recently spent a few days with Ken Blanchard, author of *The One Minute Manager*, and I had the opportunity to thank him for his support, encouragement, and the difference he has made in my life. He not only inspired me by the way he lived his life, but also by the way he encouraged me as a writer and speaker. Who will you encourage today? Be that person who someone will call five, ten, or twenty years from now and say, "Thank you. I couldn't have done it without you."

A Legacy of Purpose—People are most energized when they are using their strengths and talents for a purpose beyond themselves. To leave a legacy of purpose, make your life about something bigger than you. While you're not going to live forever, you can live on through the legacy you leave and the positive impact you make in the world.

A Legacy of Love—I often think about my mom, who passed away four years ago, and when I think about her I don't recall her faults and mistakes or the disagreements we had. After all, who is perfect? But what I remember most about her was her love for me. She gave me a legacy of love that I

now share with others. Share a legacy of love and
it will embrace generations to come.

As you read Ben Newman's book I know you will be more
inspired than ever to leave a powerful legacy. Ben and I share
many similarities on our paths of life and we connect deeply
on this concept of legacy. We both know that life is temporary but the legacy you leave is eternal. For this reason I'm
excited that Ben has delivered a life-changing message in the
form of a story that will drive you to think differently about
your life and embrace the story of the legacy you are writing.
The title of this powerful story so appropriately reminds us,
leave YOUR legacy.

—**Jon Gordon,**
Wall Street Journal bestselling author of *The Energy Bus*

Acknowledgments

Writing books is a significant part of my legacy, and I am well aware that books are not written alone. Along this journey, many people have been tremendously supportive advocates. Special gratitude goes out to my greatest team, who makes all of this possible: my family. I love you. Ami, J. Isaac, and Kennedy Rose.

I would also like to acknowledge our Director of Marketing, Kimberly Raasch, whose daily commitment to greatness helps us continue to fight and impact the thousands of lives we touch each year. And Lisa Roberts, my esteemed editor, who is truly incredible. Your commitment, passion, eagle eye, writing, and attention to detail have made this book what it is today. I cannot thank you enough.

Additionally, the opportunity to inspire and empower others through my writing would not be possible without the stories told and impact made by Dr. Jason Selk, Jon Gordon, John O'Leary, Scott Underwood, Joey Davenport, Shep Hyken, Todd Basler, Dr. Edward M. Johnson Jr.,

Lieutenant Commander Bob Gassoff, Dr. Martha Skinner, Aeneas Williams, Will Compton, Mark Daly, Andy Kaiser, Josh Qualy, Brian Cohen, Eddie Caldwell, Josh Goodman, Heath Beam, Paul Foster, Ben Beshear, Michael Kennedy Jr., Andy Parham, Adam Loewy, Laura Pierz, Michael Roberts, Scott Scully, Mark Branca, the Pranger family, the Goellner family, Teri Griege, Michael Gebben, my brother Drew Newman, my sister Sophie Newman, my paternal great grandparents Wolf and Sophie Newman, my paternal grandparents, Marcel and Bessie Newman, and to my maternal grandparents, Herman and Shirley Fishman.

A special thank-you to my father, Burt Newman, for your lessons of courage and perseverance, along with countless other family and friends who inspire me to keep fighting.

To my mother, Janet Fishman Newman; you continue to inspire me every day to be the best I can be. You taught me life's greatest lesson of LEGACY, to cherish every day . . . *Because it is not how long you live, but how you choose to live your life!*

A Note from the Author

The year was 1936 in Rüsselsheim, Germany, and master shoemaker Wolf Neumann settled in to make another pair of shoes. However, this pair of shoes would be much different than any pair he had made before.

Wolf lived in Nazi Germany in the middle of the Holocaust with his wife, Sophie, and their children, Kurt, Marcel, Gertie, and Meta. Wolf desperately wanted to get his family out of harm's way and take them to the United States to experience freedom and release from the daily worry of being killed by the Nazis.

Wolf knew he had to plan for his family's escape. First, he identified a ship that could transport his family to the United States. Then, one afternoon, Wolf strategically designed shoes that had hollow soles. The structure of the shoes would enable Wolf to insert German 1895 20-mark gold pieces into the soles of each shoe, which he could then remove and sell once his family made it safely to the United States.

It was my great-grandfather, Wolf Neumann's (changed to Newman to Americanize our family name when they came over from Rüsselsheim) purpose and foresight that gave him the ability to design these shoes. The shoes have become the connection to every ancestor of Wolf's that now lives in the United States.

When I think of LEGACY, I think of the generations that have come before you and paved the way to your future. It then becomes your responsibility to continue that legacy and pass it on to future generations. I fight every day to leave a legacy for a brighter future for my children that they can pass on to their children, my future great-grandchildren, and beyond.

Without Wolf Neumann's foresight, what future would my family have had in the United States? That is what legacy is all about. Today, my father, Burt Newman, wears the remaining German 20-mark gold piece around his neck as a symbol of our family's legacy.

Additionally, when I connect to the concept of LEGACY, I think of my mother, Janet Fishman Newman, who taught me the greatest life lesson of all: "It's not how long you live; it's how you choose to live your life."

As a young boy, I watched my mother battle a rare disease called amyloidosis. I also watched as she unleashed her positive mental attitude onto the world through a journal that she kept throughout her medical ordeal. She recognized that she still had to lead my brother and me in order to show us that we could fight adversity and challenge to be the best we could be in our lives.

Oftentimes, my mother would receive phone calls from the Boston Medical Center and Dr. Martha Skinner, telling her that she needed to come to Boston for painful procedures. It got so bad that at one point she had to wear Jobst compression stockings around her legs to control the swelling and a mask to be able to go outside. As a single mom, divorced when I was six months old, my mother would hang up the phone and immediately pick the phone back up and call her boyfriend, Alan. My mother was focused on a solution, recognizing she was still leading my brother and me. She knew we were watching her response to adversity.

Her focus was to turn the medical trip to Boston into a family trip. Because her boys liked Chinese food, she planned visits to Chinatown. Because we liked bowling, we would go candlestick bowling. My mother made a conscious choice to focus on the positive solution rather than holding on too tightly to the negative results that she couldn't control from her prognosis.

I believe that this exemplifies for all of us "The Power to REFRAME." The next time you face adversity or challenge in your life, focus on "REFRAMING," rather than holding on too tightly or spending too much time on the negativity. Choose to always focus on a positive response to maintain a path of success.

Even though amyloidosis took my mother's life in 1986, her passion for life and courage to fight a dreadful condition is now a lesson of legacy for all of us. Her attitude amidst her adversity is proof that you can be present in the moment and never stop fighting as you write the story of your legacy.

In this book, I now pass the proverbial gold coin of our family legacy on to you as symbolism of your deeper connection to those who have come before you and the lessons they shared. It is now your opportunity to connect to the person you are destined to be as you leave YOUR legacy.

Go Do Great Things,
Ben

1

Pierce Returns

Most people live life on a path that was set

for them, too afraid to live on any other. But

once in a while people will break down

barriers and obstacles to fight to be the

person they were destined to be.

—Anonymous

Rounding the corner of the massive stone home, Pierce felt like the little red caboose. His gnarly cane chanting, "I think I can, I think I can, I think I can . . ." each time it made contact with the soft, pebbly gravel. One limp leg lugging behind an eager heart that raced ahead, dragging him inside, to where—he hoped—he would find Sarah and the kids. Pulling him toward his future. I think I can. I think I can. I think . . .

Stopping shy of the back door that led to the kitchen, Pierce caught his breath. Eleven days he had been gone. He had covered so much ground in just eleven days. And now, as keen as his heart was to see his beloved family and embark on implementing all he had learned into his life, he felt . . . *something* . . . Fear? Trepidation? Excitement? Exhilaration? All four mixed together, a fancy emotional cocktail designed by a master mixologist? He could not quite put his finger on exactly what he felt, but whatever it was, it made him want to linger with his injured leg and not rush through that door with the rest of his body. Inhaling a sharp burst of cool October air, Pierce searched his mind for an answer. Exhaling with a sigh, he shrugged off the uneasy feeling, deciding it was mere butterflies—a combination of lack of food and the excitement of seeing his beautiful wife and two children. Nothing could hold him back. He was a changed man. Fearless. *I think I can. I think I can. I think . . .*

"Daddy!" Max was the first to spot Pierce, clumsily maneuvering his cane and luggage across the threshold. Sarah slowly shifted her gaze from the stovetop where she prepared dinner; a gently spiced aroma tickled Pierce's nose, causing his mouth to water and stomach to gurgle simultaneously, as Sarah's mouth collapsed into a surprised "o" shape.

"Pierce!" She remained frozen by the stove, eyes shining at the sight of her husband. Max had already hurled himself into his father's arms, as Lila slowly, gingerly approached, eventually wrapping herself around Pierce's good leg. Max wiggled in his arms excitedly, a mop of dark brown hair flailing as he chatted animatedly about how much he missed him. Lila quietly squeezed Pierce's leg, her own special way of telling him she had missed him too. Kissing the top of her strawberry-blonde hair, he marveled at how different, yet equally perfect, each of his two children was.

"Pierce! Why didn't you tell us you were coming?" Wiping both hands on the back of her jeans before taking Pierce's unshaven face in both hands, she kissed him tenderly. Wrapping herself around him and Max, she nestled against his chest as Lila entwined her tiny fingers around her mother's slender thigh—a perfect family, neatly packaged together and tied up with a dainty strawberry-blonde bow. It felt so good to be home.

* * *

Wrapped in a soft, camel-colored cashmere shawl, Sarah tucked her feet under her hips and watched Pierce intently as he made his way down the stairs. "All down for the night." He smiled goofily, uncertain what to make of his wife's expression. It was warm, for sure, yet he felt like her eyes were boring right through him. He felt . . . naked, exposed. Then her face broke into that familiar smile. The very smile he had fallen in love with back in college, perfectly white teeth flanked by soft, full pink lips and huge dimples. Honest eyes shining, hiding nothing. Sarah. It had only been eleven days, but he ached at the sight of her.

Collapsing on the couch beside her, he took her in his arms inhaling the faint grapefruit scent of her shampoo. "What were you just thinking?" Pierce asked the shiny crown of Sarah's honey-blonde head.

"When?" She pulled away from his grip, looking directly into his eyes. *Eyes boring through me,* Pierce thought once again. *What do you see?* he wondered.

"When I was coming down the stairs," he said, searching her, trying to glimpse a reaction, only to find the same shining green pools of openness and honesty he always did when he looked at her.

Sarah burst out laughing. "I was hoping you wouldn't fall! I had no idea how I would get you up and to the hospital."

Pierce couldn't help but laugh; he feared she read his mind and saw through his façade of bravado, yet all she felt was concern, and, as usual, her concern was for him. His happiness. His health. His well-being. For *him.* "Things are going to be better. I promise you."

Sarah responded by planting a tender kiss on Pierce's tanned forehead. Unraveling her legs from under her, she stood, cocking her head to one side. "Scotch?" she offered.

Pierce thought for a moment, "How about tea?" he asked.

"Tea?" Sarah raised a perfectly manicured eyebrow.

Pierce smiled broadly, affirming his request with a nod. "Tea." Reaching a hand to Sarah, she pulled him off the couch and he trailed behind, across the sprawling family room and into kitchen.

"On the wagon?" Sarah teased as she handed Pierce a steaming mug of Earl Grey tea.

"Noooo . . . I still like a scotch. I just felt like tea." He shrugged with a wink. Sarah watched Pierce closely, a bemused expression coloring her face. Smiling at her, he carefully wrapped each finger around the ceramic mug, closed his eyes and inhaled the slightly bitter aroma. Steam curled up around his nostrils, waking them as the warmth spread across his face. Popping one eye open after about one minute of this he grinned at Sarah.

"What *are* you doing?" She could not help but laugh at his odd behavior.

"Showing you the number one thing I learned on my journey."

"Number one?"

"Number one."

"Pierce Edwards, you did not travel across the country for eleven days, meeting with four exceptional and inspiring people only to return with a lesson in the art of drinking tea!"

"Try it," he urged. "You will be amazed how centering it is!" Sighing, Sarah reluctantly reached for her mug, snaked her fingers around it and closed her eyes. She had to admit, time appeared to stand still, just for that moment.

"Okay," she said, smiling warmly, long lashes fluttering her green eyes open. "Not bad . . . but, seriously, this is the number one thing you learned? This is what has you so fired up and inspired?" Indicating the two ceramic mugs sitting on the granite island, she said, "*This* is your BIG change?"

"Noooo . . . this is literally the first—number one—thing that I learned on my journey . . . from Jon." He laughed as Sarah playfully dug her fingers into his side, a well-known weak spot.

"Okay, stinker. So, speaking of Jon, we need to send him something. He saved your life."

"He did so much more than save my life, Sarah—the guy was amazing! I learned so much from each person I encountered on my journey, but Jon—well, correction, YOU got the ball rolling by sending me on the journey. Yet I still felt resistant to it—was just going through the motions to please you, you know?" He smiled earnestly at her, hoping not to hurt her feelings. "I didn't expect any more than a brief vacation and to get you and Josh off my back, to be honest. Jon cracked me open and showed me just how much I had to learn. Jon made me *hungry*, unleashing my desire and willingness to grow and change."

Sarah smiled at Pierce. She had never heard him admit to learning anything from another person before. Not that he was a know-it-all, per se; Pierce simply seemed to have an answer for everything and was genuinely never wrong. Hearing him talk this way, she swelled with pride . . . and relief. Sending him off on this journey really had been the right thing to do.

"Scotch?" she asked again.

"Sure." He smiled, proud that he had shared his—*Jon's*—tea trick with somebody. Sarah shook her head. She knew that look, recognized a similar goofy pride on Max's face when he scored a goal at soccer or on Lila's when she got a gold star from her teacher for good work, which was often. As mature, accomplished, and successful as Pierce was, a vulnerable inner child remained within, looking for approval, and she loved him for it. Loved him for letting his guard down around her and showing it every now and then. And she suspected she loved him even more in this moment, for coming home to her and the kids so inspired and eager to make changes . . . changes that would benefit them all.

"Actually, I meditate twenty minutes a day now." Sarah stopped mid-pour, gob-smacked . . . *her* husband *meditating? Daily?* She started to speak, but merely shook her head and smiled, pouring the liquid amber in two stout rocks glasses filled with ice. "I am hoping to take it to thirty minutes by the end of next week." He was bragging now.

"Really?" She plopped onto the barstool beside him, clinked the lip of her glass to his and took a long, cold sip of Oban. Closing her eyes, she followed the smoky fluid tracing its way down her throat; a pleasant flush radiated through her body, melting each and every muscle. Popping one eye open, she looked at Pierce, "You know, it kind of works with scotch too!" Laughter filled the kitchen, and was followed by love sealed with a kiss.

"I'd carry you upstairs, but I don't think it would be very romantic—or easy—using my cane." Sarah pressed herself hard against him and kissed him again. Silently picking up both scotch glasses, she made her way toward the stairs, glancing over her shoulder to be sure Pierce was following her. And he was. As fast as his good leg and cane could hurtle him, he followed his wife up the stairs to their bedroom.

2

Humble Beginnings: Change at Home

One day your life will flash before your eyes.

Make sure it is worth watching.

—Unknown

Sleepily rolling toward Pierce's side of the bed, a hungry smile drawing across her lips, Sarah reached for him. Feeling the cold empty space where his warm body should have been startled her awake. Flinching at the blinding sun shamelessly invading their bedroom, she shielded her eyes with one hand as the other searched for her watch. The sun was so bright . . . What time was it?

"Oh my gosh!" Sarah swung both legs out of bed. Reaching for her robe, she slipped it over her shoulders, hastily tying it at the waist as she hurled herself toward the door. Sarah NEVER overslept, she had to get the kids off to school and Pierce to work . . . where the heck was Pierce anyway? Heading for the stairs, her mind running at a mile a minute, a sound stopped her in her tracks. It was coming from downstairs. Peals of laughter, rolling, high-pitched squeals of delight filled the air around her. Children's laughter, her children's laughter; there was nothing in the world quite like that sound. Descending the stairs one by one, she wanted this joyous symphony to last forever. Lingering at the bottom step, she remained out of sight for a few moments, savoring each delighted squeal as it flew from the kitchen straight to her heart.

Rounding the corner, she found two perfectly dressed children sitting at the kitchen island. Lila's hair trailed down her back in neat braids tied with blue satin ribbon. She had no idea Pierce knew how to braid hair. "Mommy!" Max spoke excitedly, chunks of pancake falling from his mouth, "Daddy is making us breakfast!" He kicked his highly polished black lace-up shoes rhythmically against the island.

"I can see that!" She smiled at her husband, clean-shaven and handsome, wearing her floral apron over his crisp white shirt and grey trousers.

"And here she is kids, the lady of the house." Placing a kitchen towel over his arm with flair, he clumsily ushered Sarah to the empty place next to Lila.

"Be careful, silly . . . where's your cane?" Pierce shrugged dramatically as she surrendered to the moment and sank down onto a barstool.

Lila looked up at Sarah, her wide eyes glistening with joy. "Mommy, do you want blueberry or chocolate chip pancakes?" Sarah leaned down to kiss her daughter's head.

"Good morning!" She ruffled Max's hair as he happily stuffed more pancake into an already full mouth. "I think," she looked at directly at Pierce, "I'll take blueberry, please."

"Blueberry it is!" Flipping the handle of the pan, he twirled it in the air, expertly catching it behind his back, much to the delight of Lila and Max, who squealed and roared all over again, Max sending tiny chunks of pancake, chocolate chip, and spittle all over the floor. Taking in the scene, Sarah wished it were Saturday . . . or even Sunday, saddened by the notion that she'd soon be running out the door, ferrying the kids to school. Pierce would be at work and she would be home alone in the big empty house, remnants of pancake batter and Max's chunks on the floor a ghostly reminder that the house had been filled with joy and laughter.

Checking her watch she went to stand. "I should get dressed, the kids need to be at school by 8:45."

Pierce placed a firm hand on her arm, urging her to take her seat. "Not before breakfast is served, milady!" Lila and Max giggled. "Besides, *I* am dropping the kids at school this morning."

"But you nev—"

Pierce held up a hand caked in batter. "Last night I emailed my company executives calling a mandatory meeting for 9:30 this morning. I don't have to be at the office much before then, allowing plenty of time to drop the kids off en route. I plan to pick them up after school, too." Lila and Max swung their heads in unison, looking up at their mother in shocked disbelief. Did they really just hear their father say that? Did Sarah?

"Pierce, you've just gotten back, I am sure you have a lot to take care of at work. I can pick the kids up—they get out at 3:30 you know?"

"I know," he said with a wink, sliding a perfectly browned pancake onto the plate in front of her.

"Who are you, and what have you done with my husband?" Sarah jested.

Placing his hand on hers, he whispered, "Go get a massage today, relax, have lunch with Belinda, go shopping. Whatever takes your fancy, but do not worry about the kids; I've got it under control."

"Me-laaaady!" Max sang out, causing them all to burst into laughter.

Sarah tucked into her pancake, happy yet cautious; how long would this last? How long *could* it last? She was thrilled Pierce was making such an extraordinary effort and wanted to offer him nothing but her love and support. On the other hand, she needed to shield her children—and Pierce—from disappointment. If he messed up, Max would bounce back, but Lila would never forgive him. Sarah knew she would have to remain vigilant . . . vigilant yet hopeful.

"Why don't you two go upstairs and wash breakfast off your face and hands before school?" She picked a crumb off Max's cheek and popped it into his mouth. Pierce and Sarah silently watched as Lila guided Max upstairs. "Brush your teeth, too," Sarah called after them.

Stacking the breakfast dishes neatly in the sink, Sarah turned to Pierce. "I'm hoping we get some more alone time tonight."

He smiled suggestively, "Really, last night wasn't enough?"

"No!" She laughed. "Well, yes . . . and no!" A rush of pink rinsed over her cheeks. "I meant that I was hoping to learn more about these people who have you so fired up. Beyond the Zen art of tea drinking, that is." She smiled.

"The Zen art of tea drinking?" Pierce hugged her from behind, nuzzling his face into her soft neck. "How you mock me!" Turning to face him, she straightened his tie. "You do not need to hear about these people, Sarah. You are going to *see* them. In me, in the changes I make. BIG changes. Starting today . . . you will see each and every one of them. I promise you."

She smiled, swallowing the urge to express her fears. Not wanting to discourage him when he was so clearly fired up.

"Thank you," she said. "For breakfast, it was a real treat. Especially for Lila and Max."

Pierce's eyes lit up, "Did you see how talkative she was, how open?"

Sarah nodded, uttering a silent prayer of hope that it would last. "So, BIG changes at the office too?" Fearing she might crack, she changed the subject to something less emotional to her.

"Oh, yeah." He nodded enthusiastically. Raising his eyebrows for emphasis, he added, "HUGE changes."

"Any doubts creeping in?" She could not imagine Pierce changing a thing at work. He had worked his ass off, building the company from scratch; it was *his* baby.

"Nope." He folded his arms across his chest, smug, defiant.

"None?" She arched her brow; a familiar and knowing expression. He shook his head, ignoring the uneasy feeling gurgling within. He was going to be fine. Change was going to be easy. Look how much he had changed already!

3

Humble Beginnings: Change at Work

If I have the belief that I can do it, I shall surely acquire the capacity to do it even if I may not have it in the beginning.

—Mahatma Gandhi

Pierce leaned against the cool glass window, watching as Lila led her younger brother through piles of orange and yellow leaves toward his preschool, a small red-brick structure to the left of the main building of Saint Joseph's Elementary. At six she seemed mature beyond her years—it could have just as easily been Sarah leading Max. His heart ached at the sight and even more at the memory of her laughing this morning. The sturdy fortress she habitually built around herself in Pierce's presence, gone. Obliterated by a simple pancake breakfast and some fancy twirling of a frying pan. Pierce knew it was so much more than those theatrics, and much simpler. It was time. He had given his children his time. It would not have mattered what he did; Pierce being there was good enough for them.

Lila rounded the corner of the glass and brick building and stopped briefly before the two large, rectangular doors leading to the elementary school building. Hesitating, she shyly lifted her hand, waving to Pierce before slipping through the doors where she was immediately swallowed by a sea of blue uniforms.

"Good-bye, Lila," he said to the glass, barely audible—stunned that she had taken the time to look for him and wave good-bye, stung that she had hesitated. He thought back to Jon and his lesson about trusting and believing in others—he glimpsed, through a tiny little crack today, that Lila could perhaps learn to believe in him again. He was regaining her trust. It felt exhilarating, yet scary, precariously tiptoeing on a tightrope . . . an extremely fragile one. "Have a great day, sweetheart," Pierce whispered to the wind as it whipped up the path, leaves dancing and flying in its wake.

Pulling away from the curb, a mess of leaves crunching beneath his tires, Pierce noticed a group of teenage boys shooting hoops in the quadrangle adjacent to Lila and Max's school. High school boys—he had forgotten Saint Joseph's recently added a middle and high school to its campus. A vague memory of a rather large and generous donation Sarah had made to the school resurfaced, her argument that the kids would have the stability of staying within the same school system, on the same campus, and with the same group of friends all the way through high-school graduation falling on deaf ears. Too busy for details, Pierce wanted only the abridged version—how much did they want, was it tax deductible, and, of course, how important was it to Sarah?

Pierce glanced at the clock on the dash—he had plenty of time to get to the office. Missing the earlier commuter rush to the city had saved him the congested, messy drama of the interstate at peak hour. As he watched the boys dribble the ball effortlessly down the court, Pierce felt carefree and relaxed and decided to pull over. Cutting the engine and alighting from the Escalade, he strolled toward a gleaming new building that could only be the new middle and high schools . . . *May as well see where my money went,* he thought to himself, struggling to recall any more details beyond writing a check. Drawing a blank, he correctly assumed Sarah had attended the grand opening without him.

Slipping his free hand into his pocket, he picked up his pace. Still relatively warm for late October, the wind was laced with an unforgiving bite. Drawing closer he could see the new building was beautiful, and even though he had had no hand in its design—in fact, had forgotten it existed, or that BlackBird Tech had funded a large portion of it— he felt a surge of pride. Aware he could take no credit for its aesthetics, he realized he had made a mark in his community, had done something for the greater good. Albeit without acknowledging or really caring about it at the time, *and* with Sarah's relentless urging, but it filled him with a glorious mix of pride and hope. Hope that, with his new attitude and desire for change, he would accomplish greater things.

Hobbling back to the Escalade, a smile plastered across his face, he lost his reverie to the cheering of the boys. Looking up, he marveled at a lanky brunette kid swinging from the hoop, completing a spectacular slam-dunk, his delighted brethren whooping and cheering him on. Their youth, enthusiasm, and passion immediately conjured Coach Edwards to the forefront of his mind.

Coach E. Pierce smiled at the memory of this remarkable man. What a character! The boys he had dedicated his life to coaching were not much older than the five boys in front of Pierce right now. In his mind's eye, he imagined Coach E. on the court with them, playing as eagerly and robustly as a sixteen-year-old, his rugged face flushed with an infectious joy, encouraging the boys to start their day positively. What was the coach's big thing, aside from his passion for basketball? He had a *passion* for the *process*. YOUR Prizefighter Day, that's what he had called it. Stuffing his hands deeper in his pockets, Pierce turned away from the image of his mentor gleefully playing ball with the live flesh-and-blood boys in front of him and purposefully made his way back to the car. It was time to begin his Prizefighter Day. He had wondered how and when he would incorporate it into his routine, and now seemed like the perfect moment.

* * *

Sliding behind the steering wheel, he pressed the start button and allowed the car to idle, warmth from the heaters immediately merging with his cool breath, forging a light layer of steam on the windows. Reaching for his treasured black notebook, he leafed through it until he came across Coach E.'s exercise, scrawled on a flimsy restaurant napkin. Pierce made a mental note to have his secretary, Sabina, type it up neatly. In fact, he would have her type each exercise and technique shared by his mentors and print copies to give his staff at the board meeting later that morning. Pressing his foot on the accelerator, Pierce became eager to get to the office and ignite the same burning fire in his staff that he felt in the pit of his gut! Things were going to be GREAT!

Driving on an uncongested interstate was pure joy! Pierce could not believe he had not discovered this earlier in life— why fight traffic if you can leave a little later and avoid it altogether? By his calculation, he would arrive at the office only fifteen minutes later than he would have had he left home an hour earlier! Saving him, what?—forty-five minutes of stressed-out honking, crawling, and brake tapping . . . even longer in the event of a pileup or breakdown, neither of which was uncommon.

Elated, he looked directly at himself in the rearview mirror and asked, "Are you ready to make this YOUR Prizefighter Day?" Immediately the three activity goals he had targeted for the day sprang to mind, and, realizing he had already achieved two of them and was well on his way to achieving the third—all before 9:00 a.m.—he relished how easy it was. Steering the Escalade toward the exit ramp of the interstate, he checked them off one by one.

Personal Goal: Twenty minutes of meditation and a quick workout before the kids and Sarah awake. Check! In fact, he had surpassed it. Rising at 4:30 a.m., he successfully extended his meditation to a good solid thirty minutes before hitting the weight room in the basement for an hour. He felt victorious!

Service to Others: A daily random act of kindness. Well, that was easy—he had given Sarah a break by cooking breakfast and preparing the kids for and dropping them off at school. A twinge of guilt ripped through his chest; Sarah was, after all, his wife. Should he really view sharing the load of family life with her as service? Recollecting leaning across her naked body, tangled in the massive duvet and soft cream sheets, to switch off her alarm that morning, he affirmed that he had, in his own way, been of service to her. When did Sarah last sleep in—not only on a weekday—but a weekend too? Certainly not since they had the kids, and prior to that, she herself had worked long, crazy hours at a busy city law firm.

Shame washed over him at the thought of all Sarah had

given up for the sake of their family. A highly successful defense attorney, she had walked away from it all to devote herself to their family and support Pierce on his own path to success. Pierce knew it was Sarah who deserved the praise for selfless service and not him for simply turning off her lousy alarm, allowing her a mere *one* out of *thousands* of mornings to lie in. Shrugging off remorse, he asserted that, for him, it was at least a good start. So, check!

Business Goal: Daily act of intentional leadership. Call board meeting and restructure the company. Deconstruct the corporate pyramid to build a team of equally invested leaders. Check! The board meeting had been called, and he was on his way to deliver the news to his staff and make the sweeping changes he deemed necessary. Loosely mapping out his thoughts on how it should be handled in his home office that morning before waking the kids, he knew some staff might view the changes as a demotion. He needed to tread carefully, making it clear that skilled leadership was expected and salaries would remain commensurate with that.

In fact, for many, salary would essentially improve. *Awesome*, he thought. *Double goal!* Mentally checking off yet another service goal with a deep sense of smug satisfaction, he patted himself on the back for yet another display of pure altruism: being of *service* to his staff and single-handedly establishing easier and better work and home environments for his employees.

And, if Sabina could type as fast as he knew she could, he would be introducing his team leaders to the wisdom of Coach E., Jon Davis, Lieutenant J. Bobby Rehnquist, and Dr. Rose Barnes in that very meeting—impacting lives and placing each and every leader on their own path to personal greatness.

Taking a deep breath, he felt like a superhero. This stuff truly was empowering.

Checking his reflection in the mirror once again, he smiled. Change was *good*. Feeling the effects already, via his exceptionally calm and relaxed demeanor, he began to *see* them in the image echoed back to him. The tranquil face staring from the mirror uncannily resembled Jon's, super-chilled and peaceful. It was astonishing how effective and powerful change was—only this morning he had boldly promised Sarah that she would "see" each of these remarkable people in him, but he did not realize he would be seeing them too. Not so clearly, nor so quickly.

4

Humble Beginnings: Old Behaviors Return

Courage is rightly esteemed the first of human qualities . . . because it is the quality which guarantees all others.
—Winston Churchill

Pulling into his reserved space, conveniently located next to a bank of elevators that would carry him directly to his offices, Pierce looked at the metal sign on the wall with contempt: "CEO Pierce Edwards." Shiny, stuffy letters preventing anybody who did not bear his name and title from taking possession of this small rectangular space of grey cement. Did anybody else in his organization have assigned parking? Pierce could not be sure, but taking stock of his surroundings, he failed to locate another metal nametag attached to the concrete walls. He wondered if Anderson had used this space during his absence, knowing full well that he would not have. Taking in the abundance of convenient parking spaces available, the sign on the wall was strong evidence of Pierce's inflated ego; he would have it removed by the end of the day. Starting tomorrow, just like everybody else in his organization, Pierce would drive in and choose any old parking space each morning.

"Good morning, Sabina," he sang out to his secretary, stopping directly in front of her desk and looking her straight in the eye.

"G-good morning, Mr. Edwards." Sabina flushed crimson. Pierce had never greeted her on his way in—he was usually talking on his phone. "Welcome back." She smiled nervously and glanced at her watch, shocked to see it was almost 9:15a.m. Didn't he have a board meeting scheduled in fifteen minutes? "I-I-I prepared the board room for you. I do hope I have the time correct?"

"Ah, yes," Pierce said, looking at his watch. "9:30 meeting; I should get a move on. Thank you, Sabina." He winked and smiled before walking toward the heavy wood doors segregating his office from hers. Sabina's big round eyes followed him, her mouth hanging open as her tiny, astounded ears scrambled to place the foreign sound registering in the air. Was that *whistling* she heard? Coming from her *boss*? In the ten years she had worked for Pierce Edwards she had never heard him whistle, sing, or display emotion—other than rage when things were not going his way. Not that that was common—Pierce typically locked himself in his office, quietly and diligently working, speaking on the phone, or holed up in meetings—it seemed there was rarely moment to spare for him to display emotion. But the few times he had, and she had borne witness, it was almost always when something had gone wrong and he was looking for somebody to blame.

Sinking into his large, soft leather chair, Pierce leaned back, closed his eyes and breathed in the smell of his office—the distinct blend of leather mixed with cedar. A passion for books inspired custom-built, cedar-lined units to be designed for his office; the smell had never faded. Safely wrapped in the powerful embrace of his firm leather seat, he felt dominant. Quickly snapping his eyes open, he began to search for signs of Anderson. Like a spoiled, jealous child who cannot bear to share his toys, he studied his desk closely. Not a thing had been moved; even his pencil cup was stocked and positioned exactly the way Pierce liked it. It contained one eraser-tipped pencil, two Sharpies, a highlighter, and a fine-point Uni-ball pen and sat to the right of a heavily lacquered frame that housed a cheerful portrait of Sarah and the kids. Reaching effortlessly for the Uni-ball pen, Pierce could tell the cup had not been moved; he dropped the pen back in the cup with a disappointed clunk. Pierce glided the top drawer of his mahogany desk open and glanced inside. His Montblanc pen, a gift from Sarah, smiled back at him. It was evident that Anderson had not used his office during his brief tenure, and Pierce could not understand why this disappointed him; angered him a little, even. Why was he looking to pick a fight?

Looking around his office, he began to connect the dots. Large and pretentious, his surroundings cried power and solitude at once. Anderson had not *wanted* to use this office, and Pierce grappled to face two cold, hard truths as they arose in his consciousness:

ONE: Anderson was way more skilled and advanced in terms of capability and leadership skills than Pierce gave him credit for. Emotionally mature and balanced, he did not *need* to wear Pierce's proverbial shoes in order to get the job done. He parked where he normally parked, sat where he normally sat, and got the job done—and got it done well. Not once, it appeared, did he allow his ego to get excited and *act* like the boss, playing dress-up in Pierce's office as Pierce had childishly imagined.

And, TWO: Sitting in his pompous office and breathing its familiar smells, the powerful effect of sense memory had taken a momentary grip on Pierce. The rush of the familiar had conjured the "old" Pierce, like a gypsy with a Ouija board calling back lost spirits. Laughing to himself, he felt grateful once again for the opportunity to change and even more so for this keen insight. It was going to take awareness and hard work to keep his old habits in check, especially in surroundings where the habits where so deeply ingrained—an impossibly stubborn stain in a fine silk carpet.

The buzzing intercom on his desk shattered his thoughts. It was Sabina, alerting him that most of the management team had signed in and entered the boardroom. "Thank you, Sabina; I am on my way." Stopping by her desk on his way to the boardroom, he dropped the notes from his journey in front of her. "Would you mind typing these up for me, Sabina? Oh, and separate them out, a new page for each person's lessons." Sabina looked puzzled, mainly because Pierce never *asked* her if she minded doing anything, but merely gave curt orders. Pierce understood her expression to mean she did not under-stand his instructions. "Don't worry, each exercise is clearly marked and labeled . . . Pop in to the boardroom with copies for everybody once you're done, okay?"

"Sure," Sabina nodded shakily after a long beat, stunned that Pierce waited around for her answer. "Oh—Mr. Edwards?" she called after him, stopping Pierce in his tracks. Did she really just call him that? Turning, he took in her frizzy grayish hair and heavy spectacles; she looked to be in her early sixties, which meant she was close to twenty years his senior. And she called him Mr. Edwards, not Pierce? How long had she worked for him, he wondered? Had she started calling him that of her own free will and had he, arrogantly, not bothered to correct her? Or, worse, had he insisted upon making a lady, old enough to be his own mother, call him Mr. Edwards just because he considered her to be his subordinate? He shuddered at the thought. "Pierce," he said firmly.

"E-ex-, er, pardon me?" Sabina, having stood up from her desk, timidly stepped back, her face reddening once again.

"Pierce, call me Pierce, Sabina." He flashed a reassuring smile before turning back toward the boardroom.

"Oh . . . er . . . oh . . . Mr. Ed-errr . . . ummm, oh dear . . . Pierce?" Stumbling over her words, Sabina barely caught his attention in time.

"Yes, Sabina?"

"Er, did you need me to call Anderson Phillips? I did not see his name on the list and I noticed he was not copied on the email last night." The fact that she had called Anderson by his full name, and not Mr. Phillips, did not go unnoticed by Pierce, much to his chagrin. Taking a moment to move past his insecurities and focus on the task at hand, he could not believe this oversight. How did he manage to exclude Anderson from the meeting?

"It's okay, Sabina. Thanks, I will take care of it." Crossing the wide room with Jon's cane bouncing against the hard cherrywood floors, he returned to his office and dialed Anderson's extension on speakerphone.

"Anderson Phillips." Anderson's calm voice filled the office.

"Anderson. Pierce Edwards."

"Pierce, great to hear your voice! Welcome back."

"Thanks. Listen, I know it's short notice, but I've called an executive meeting in the boardroom this morning to review company structure. Obviously, I will need you there."

"Sure. What time?"

Pierce felt a white-hot heat flush his neck and face. Loathing transparency, he knew Anderson would catch the oversight; swallowing fears he firmly ordered, "Now."

"I'm sorry, Pierce. I have a conference call scheduled in five minutes."

"Cancel it." Pierce snapped, his tone catching both men by surprise.

"Once again, Pierce, I am very sorry, but I can't do that." Anderson's tone remained calm yet he was shaken by the sudden and intense return of his boss. "We're down to working out the finer points on the Nabhas deal and have scheduled a conference call with the team in India at 7 p.m. local time to discuss the merger. It is imperative I be on that call, Pierce; orchestrating the merger over the coming weeks needs to be carefully monitored if it is to be seamless."

Pierce knew Anderson was right. It was his own fault Anderson had not been made aware of the meeting in a timely manner. And apparently, had Anderson been included in last night's email, he would have been unable to commit to the meeting. Still, Pierce loathed the spiraling, free-falling sensation of power and influence slipping from his grip.

"Fine, Anderson, I understand." He half-barked, "Stop by the boardroom once you're done. Today is a BIG day for Black-Bird Tech. Some BIG—very big—changes are imminent."

"O-kay." Anderson thought for a moment, before gently yet firmly speaking his mind. "Pierce, all due respect, buddy. But do you think it is wise to make changes prior to the merger? Perhaps we should allow the dust to settle after the merger takes place, and then implement changes . . . especially if they are big changes as you are suggesting?"

Pierce fumed. Who did Anderson Phillips think he was, telling him how to run his own damn company? Responding slowly and carefully, through gritted teeth, he worked extremely hard to conceal the anger and contempt charging through him.

"All due respect, Anderson, I have thought long and hard about my decisions and feel very ready to implement change for our operation. Stop by the boardroom once your call is done. And set some time aside this afternoon to bring me up to speed on the Nabhas deal." He cut the speakerphone off before Anderson could respond and slammed his palm on the desk, finally setting the violent torrent of anger free.

Leaning forward on his desk, Pierce buried his head in his hands. The chipper mood that had followed him all morning spun wildly away along with his sense of control. "Damn it!" he cursed, slamming his hand against the desk once again. He despised the fact that Anderson's point had made complete sense. Massaging his temples, Pierce took three long, deliberate breaths, composing himself before stepping out of the office.

Sabina waved from where she stood by the copy machine. "Mr.— Pierce, I typed those exercises up for you. I'm running off copies now and will bring them in shortly." She smiled. He had no idea how many words per minute she managed, but Sabina typed like Superman on steroids. Many secretaries would still be sitting behind their desks filing their nails, the younger ones glued to social media on their boss's time. He wondered what he paid her and made a mental note to review her salary package.

"Thanks, Sabina. You're the best." He offered a little salute in her direction before stepping inside the boardroom, where the busy hum of chatter dimmed to silence as Pierce took his seat at the head of an excessively long glass table. Immediately noticing the contradiction, he made a contrived show of moving to a seat at the middle of the table, positioning himself between Jane Evans, chief sustainability officer and BlackBird Tech's sole female executive, and Anuj Verma, chief technology officer. Pierce smiled broadly at his executive team.

Eleven men and one woman made up the team. Pierce sat at the top as CEO and president. Second in charge, Anderson Phillips served as vice president. Then came four chiefs, one general manager, and five directors—each oversaw multiple layers of management and staff, from engineering to janitorial. ALL eyes fixed on Pierce, waiting for him to speak.

"Good morning, everyone!" Muffled *good mornings* politely rippled around the room, a subservient echo bouncing off the walls. "First of all, I appreciate you taking the time to attend this meeting on such short notice." He paused for effect, "Secondly, congratulations to those who worked closely with Anderson Phillips in my absence. As you know, the Nabhas deal was negotiated during this period, and a merger will be taking place over the coming weeks." This time around, gentle murmur of chatter felt slightly charged as the foreign notion of praise registered with the team.

"My dream for BlackBird Tech has long been to grow it from the largest aerospace technology company in the country to one of the largest globally. We," he flapped his hand, gesturing around the room, "are inching closer to attaining this goal. Currently, Nabhas supplies the majority of Southeast Asian and Australian commercial markets as well as approximately one-third of Western Europe, in addition to long-standing government contracts with the Australian and New Zealand defense forces. Once Nabhas is merged with BlackBird Tech, we will be actively supplying flight technology to over fifty countries along with four government defense contracts—Australia, New Zealand, the United States, and Canada. Visions for growth beyond the merger include expansion to 30 percent more new countries and territories, in addition to successful bids on government contracts within the UK and Western Europe within the first five years."

The team began to relax. Most had found Pierce's email unnerving—a short rant about dramatically restructuring the company and an all-executive meeting on short-to-zero notice had reeked suspiciously of layoffs. Now it appeared their fears were unjustified—he merely wanted to boost morale and highlight the possibility of upcoming role changes to accommodate the merger and subsequent growth.

Feeling at ease, Will Simpson, director of human resources, surrendered to a daydream of being transferred to southern France to headhunt new talent within continental Europe . . . or perhaps Munich would be more central.

"So far, we have been successful," Pierce said, waving around the table once again, "with our current corporate structure in place." Pounding his fist on the table dramatically, he shouted, "I believe we can be better!" Anuj and Jane flinched. And Will, catapulted from the cobblestone streets of Munich back to the boardroom of BlackBird Tech in Charlotte, North Carolina, snapped his pencil in half.

Pierce spread out a diagram of BlackBird Tech's corporate pyramid on the table in front of him. Smoothing it with his large tanned hands, he smiled at the apprehensive faces suspended around the table. Time had stopped for each person in the room, except Pierce, who cleared his throat and continued, "As of today, the chart on this piece of paper has no meaning."

Gerry Lowitz, CFO, widened his eyes at John Paul Baxter, the quiet yet effective COO sitting across from him. John Paul subtly shook his head and lowered his eyes. He had no idea what was coming, but he knew that with a major merger in the works, any form of distraction or detour from the task at hand could be severely detrimental.

Rapping his knuckles on the pyramid, Pierce joked, "I see a lot of chiefs here! Chief executive, chief operations . . . sustainability . . . technology. Directors, too . . . engineering, marketing, admin, HR . . . And then we have Kang Chen, general manager." Kang smiled nervously, shifting in his seat. "Is this a case of too many head chefs in the kitchen?" The muffled murmur danced around the room once again, carrying with it the unmistakable high-pitched note of alarm.

Raising his palm in the air to silence the room, Pierce smiled even wider. The wider he smiled the tighter the knot in Kang Chen's stomach became, and, glancing around the table, Kang sensed his colleagues felt no different. "What we have here has been working, I understand. It has been effective, yes. But I know it can be better, and I plan to show you how." Sabina sneaked in, silently placing a pile of papers in front of Pierce. Glancing down, he noticed she had separated each exercise out and clipped them together in neat booklets; placing them aside for the moment, he continued.

"Each of us in this room, myself included, is effectively managing. There is no denying that. But are we effectively *leading*?" He waited, allowing his rhetoric to marinate. Speaking softly now he emphasized his point, "Are we *managing* or are we *leading*?" The room fell silent.

"Jane?" Turning to the attractive brunette sitting to his right, he asked, "Are you really the CHIEF sustainability officer, or are you the sustainability *leader*?" Jane's angular bob did little to hide her discomfort at being put on the spot in front of her peers. "Lucas, are you the DIRECTOR of engineering or the engineering *team leader*?" Jane relaxed as the attention shifted to Lucas Webb, who nervously backed his glasses further up the bridge of his nose.

Pierce pushed his chair away from the table, extended his legs in front of him and reclined back, cradling his head in his hands. "BlackBird Tech no longer has chiefs. We do not have directors." He looked toward Kang, "And we do not have managers. What we *do* have are *leaders* who work together, leading each team member from our top software programmer to our stockroom clerk, combining our talents, and running a company where each individual is proudly and professionally vested.

"From this moment on, I will be stepping down as chief executive officer. You will be stepping down from your current titles and roles." Pierce waited as the murmur whipped around the room once again, panicked hands of drowning people frantically scrambling to send an S.O.S.

"Each of you will be reappointed as team leaders of your respective divisions. Serving as board members, we will unite to weigh in on decisions regarding company operations as one team, regardless of our areas of expertise."

John Paul raised his hand, "I notice Anderson Phillips is not present. Will he be stepping in as CEO?"

"Good question, J.P. Anderson had a conflict this morning and will be joining us as soon as he can. Unfortunately for him," Pierce chuckled at his own joke, "the CEO position is no longer taking applications." Nervous laughter mixed in with the murmur—nobody was quite sure exactly what this meant for Anderson. His absence from the meeting's email request did not go unnoticed by anybody in the room. Only Pierce knew it was a genuine oversight, or a Freudian slip—of that even he could not be certain.

"My goal is to do away with hierarchy and titles and build

a solid, dependable team. I trust each and every one of you in your roles as they have been defined to this point, but I see more potential for the company if we break down role-defining barriers and work together on an equal plane. This includes the staff from each department. I am requesting each division be restructured in the following manner: appoint managers to team leadership roles and work closely with these leaders to explore the strengths of each team member, redefining individual roles according to these strengths. I do not want any employee—excuse me, *team member*—to feel they work *for* somebody as opposed to *with* them.

"Any questions?"

"Without a CEO, I assume, as the owner, we will ultimately continue to report and answer to you, Pierce?" John Paul, once again, plucked up the courage to speak.

"No. No, you won't, J.P. Sure, my presence will remain here at BlackBird as chairman of the board; Anderson Phillips will be my co-chair. Any major decisions the board gets stuck on, Anderson and I will work with you to resolve, but, ultimately, each of you, as BlackBird Tech's board of directors, will be the driving force behind the company." At that moment, Anderson Phillips slipped in the door. Tall and thin, he easily slid past the first few chairs and sat in the empty seat between Ethan Williams and Hugo Marshall. His arrival palpably shifted the atmosphere's energy; the entire room felt at ease.

"Apologies, everyone." Anderson smiled. Taking in the confused expressions, he asked, "What did I miss?"

"Oh, you know . . . demotions and pay cuts," Hugo, the former director of marketing half-joked.

"Anderson, you are right on time—we were about to brainstorm our new company purpose statement." Pierce felt excited at the prospect of sharing his thoughts on this, inspired by none other than Lieutenant J. Bobby Rehnquist and Navy SEAL protocol. "But before we do, why don't we take a quick break? I need to stretch my bum knee."

"Pierce, one comment, if I may, before we move on to other affairs." John Paul sat up a little straighter; it seemed he had more confidence in Anderson's presence.

"Sure," Pierce, standing now, reached for Jon's cane and shifted his weight between his good and bad leg. Sitting for more than thirty minutes at a stretch left his injured leg feeling numb.

"While I certainly see the restructuring you propose as valid, may I suggest, for continuity's sake, we hold off and revisit this once the merger with Nabhas is complete and running smoothly?" Anderson immediately looked to John Paul; having no idea exactly what changes Pierce proposed in his absence, he recognized the shared sentiment. Heck, it did not matter what the changes were; now was not the time to change anything.

Watching Pierce hop from one leg to the other, desperately trying to get the feeling back, Anderson regretted ending his conference call. As it turned out, twenty minutes into the call, his own meeting had come to a halt. Unable to continue strategic discussions regarding the integration of Nabhas and BlackBird internal software systems to one central hub without chief tech officer Anuj on the call, Anderson found himself making a feeble excuse and rescheduling. Now he found himself utterly perplexed as to why he and Anuj—*why anybody*—were here now rather than working on the biggest deal in BlackBird's history.

"As a team, I am confident we can handle all of the changes very easily." Pierce turned and hobbled off toward the bathrooms down the hall. "We'll reconvene in ten minutes," he shouted over his shoulder. "And may I ask you all to bring back a mug of hot tea? Even if you don't drink tea."

Puzzled looks were exchanged behind Pierce's back. Anderson sank down into his chair and buried his face in his hands. Blindsided and confused, he felt like he had just entered the twilight zone. Pierce had failed to inform him about the meeting, and now there was all this talk about restructuring the company without consulting him beforehand. J.P.'s urging Pierce to hold off also profoundly worried Anderson. Begrudgingly he rose and fixed himself a mug of peppermint tea.

Nobody spoke, Blackberries and iPhones were consulted, meetings and schedules pushed back, and a few curious looks were exchanged across the table. Mugs of hot tea were dutifully prepared and brought to the table, yet nobody spoke a word to each other.

Pierce hobbled back into the room, shuffled the papers Sabina had left earlier, and cleared his throat. Glancing around, he took mental stock of his team, each with a steaming mug placed in front of them. Good.

"I see you all have your tea," he said, smiling broadly. "I want us to spend some time working *together*—as the newly appointed board of directors—to redefine our company purpose statement. But before we begin, I wanted to share a little centering exercise I picked up from somebody much wiser than myself." He smiled again—bigger this time. Nobody smiled back.

Anderson silently prayed for strength. He knew how hard each person sitting at this table was working to meet the requirements and deadline for the merger. Nobody had *time* for a freaking tea party, nor to rewrite a purpose statement— these things could wait! Fear kept them firmly rooted to their seats, humoring their unpredictable boss. Yet the loathing could be felt, a palpable surge charging the room. Wrestling the urge to speak out, Anderson knew if they could just suffer through this meeting and get back to the task at hand, they would succeed. If Pierce truly was allowing the entire executive team to have an equal voice as board of directors, they would be able to band together and get the job done. *Yes,* Anderson decided, *let's humor Pierce and get this meeting over with so we can all get back to work and get the job done.* Stepping down as CEO, Pierce knew it was time to be getting out of their way. Anderson's anger subsided as he began to realize that the changes proposed really could be for the better.

Once Pierce had talked everybody through the Zen art of tea drinking, he passed out the exercises Sabina had typed up—one for each team member. He proudly looked on as each of his board of directors leafed through the four pages in front of them:

Page One: "Attaining Belief in Yourself"—Jon Davis

Page Two: "Acting with Courage and Integrity"—Lieutenant J. Bobby Rehnquist

Page Three: "YOUR Prizefighter Day"—Coach Todd Edwards

Page Four: "Creating a Living Legacy"—Dr. Rose Barnes

"Refer to page two." Pierce commanded, and the team dutifully opened to page two:

Acting with Courage and Integrity—Lieutenant J. Bobby Rehnquist

- Identify the truth and act from there with courage and integrity.
- TEAM WORK – Ego is I, Team is WE
- Appreciate all people and the selfless acts and sacrifices they make daily.
- SEAL motto: *The only easy day was yesterday.*

"This is the motto of the Navy SEAL: The only easy day was yesterday." Pierce allowed the words to hang in the air.

You can say that again, Anderson thought—as did many others in the room.

Pierce beamed with pride as he read from the page in front of him, "*Team work. Ego is I, TEAM is WE.* Something else I learned from a brief conversation with a Navy SEAL. I want our company philosophy to reflect this. I want our purpose statement to reflect this. I want to believe in the GREATNESS and POWER of WE. I want each and every team member to believe in this and every client and potential client to know they have an entire TEAM on their side when they engage BlackBird Technologies."

Glancing up to the current purpose statement—emblazoned on a plaque mounted high on the wall—Pierce read aloud, "Revolutionizing the aviation industry through innovative thinking, superior research, technology, and customer service." Pointing his index finger in its general direction he added, "I like it . . . I have to, I wrote it! But I don't *love* it. It does not fire me up. It does not make me feel I am part of a great team, and I doubt it fires up any of our employees—excuse me—*team members*. What are your thoughts, Hugh? You are the leader of marketing, and your expertise is in engaging people. Will, I'd like your thoughts too—HR has intimate knowledge of team members. What fires them up, Will?"

Will cleared his throat, "In all honesty, I like the current purpose statement."

Hugh nodded in agreement, "The message is short, concise, and to the point. We *have* revolutionized the aviation industry and plan to do so on a global scale. We are right on point with our purpose statement; this alone should keep team members fired up and on track."

"Good, Hugh, but it is not about maintenance; your point reiterates the need for change if we've achieved our mission. We need to continue to grow. It's like graduating high school with honors—a moment of glory—but now it is time for college. If you want to graduate summa cum laude, the work has only just begun.

"We're more effective as a team, and the company purpose statement needs to reflect this idea in order to inspire it. Any ideas?" Pierce glanced around the table, his eyes settling on Kang Chen, who shifted uncomfortably in his seat. "Kang, you've been general manager for how long?"

"Five years, sir."

"General manager . . . I guess you will be general *leader* now." Pierce smiled, "Doesn't have much of a ring to it, does it? Never mind, we will come up with something catchy for you. As *general manager,* you've overseen many divisions and a multitude of staff. Now, as general *leader*, you will oversee many teams and a multitude of team members. What do *you* think will invoke team spirit?"

Catching on to Pierce's unity theme, and desperately wanting to keep his job, Kang carefully altered the purpose statement: "Revolutionizing global aviation through unity, innovation, superior technology, research, and customer service."

Pierce nodded, "Good, good . . . but, I think we can do better than simply adding a word or two to the current statement. Any other thoughts?" Kang lowered his eyes, fearing his position would vanish as quickly as his title.

"Our purpose statement should be as easily recognizable as the Navy SEAL trident. I propose we give it three distinct prongs: TEAMWORK, INNOVATION, and INTEGRITY." Pierce held three fingers up in the air, emphasizing his point,

"Revolutionizing the global aviation industry with TEAM-WORK, INNOVATION, and INTEGRITY. Those three key words will be all caps, all the time. Take this philosophy back and drive it into your teams today. Destruct the pyramids of hierarchy within your respective divisions, and develop teams of experts who will work together with this philosophy at their core. Call on each other for help and support as you implement change, and know that Anderson and I are available for guidance should you need our support. Any questions?"

Once again, nobody spoke. What could they possibly say? Pitched as a roundtable meeting, it was anything but a full circle. Evidently the only thing it revolved around, no matter how well intended, were Pierce's new ideals and his relentless mission to implement them.

"Let's meet again tomorrow at 9:30 a.m. to discuss the transformation as it occurs and address any questions or issues that arise as a team. This will also allow me the opportunity to share some pretty amazing stuff with you all." Pierce smiled warmly, rapping his knuckles on the remaining three pages of wisdom carefully copied, collated, and clipped by Sabina.

Attaining Belief in Yourself—Jon Davis

- Great leaders believe in others. To believe in others, one must first believe in self.
- Use meditation and mindfulness to gain focus and clarity—slowing down and thinking before acting.
- Act with purpose, intention, and awareness at all times.
- Use following method for attaining belief in self:

Five Key Factors for Attaining Belief in Yourself

1. Accept the truth: Realizing and identifying with the person you are today is the key to becoming the person you want to be. We never actually fail in life, we just don't always get the results that we want. You can no longer live a lie. You have to acknowledge and identify with what is most important in your life and ultimately attain belief in yourself.

2. Speak the truth: Because there is regret from your past behavior and habits, you may be terrified to talk about it or acknowledge it. This only serves to amplify the pain and make us feel like victims. Get the truth out into the light. Talk about your experience with a trusted friend or a professional.

3. Breathe through the truth: Even though every fiber of your being wants to react and believe that your actions up to this point have been correct, know that you can change. Avoid acting from a place of pain or anger. The best way to reclaim your dignity is to act rationally and treat yourself lovingly. Do not self-destruct.

4. Process the truth: Give yourself time and space to find your equilibrium. Believe confidently and wholeheartedly that along with change you will develop a stronger foundation. Recognize that this will take time. Give yourself that time.

5. Create a plan based on the truth: Don't expect things to be perfect right away by flipping a switch and having a new life. Old behaviors and mindsets often come back into the realm. Stay strong and acknowledge that you must continue to believe and actively engage in this process in order to experience concrete change for your future. With this in mind, define how you want to live your life from now on.

Take out a piece of paper and write down any idea about the person you want to be and the life you want to live. Once you have clarity on this, you can take concrete steps toward realizing your goals and attaining belief in yourself.

YOUR Prizefighter Day—Coach Todd Edwards

- Be willing to put other people before you. Be willing to be of service to others.
- GDGT!—*Go do GREAT things!*
- Set attainable daily activities—personal, business, and service—and make each day VICTORIOUS. YOUR Prizefighter Day.

YOUR Prizefighter Day

The key: Identify three things that are activity-driven for you and your life that if you accomplish today, makes today victorious (regardless of any obstacles that come your way). Hearing from individuals from around the country who have successfully implemented these ongoing goals, they've chosen one that's personal, one that's business- or athletic-related, and one that's all about helping someone else:

1. **Personal activity example:** waking up every morning and getting in your morning workout because it makes you feel good (endorphins) and confident (strong) about your ability to go out and do great things.

2. **Business-related example (in a sales career):** setting a specific goal for the number of phone calls that you have to make every day knowing (regardless of the results) that will further your business and your success. Athletic-related example: following through in the daily process of studying your playbook, completing your workout, and making the right choices with your daily nutrition.

3. **Example of being in service of another:** random act of kindness for another (i.e., buying a cup of coffee anonymously for the next person in line at the coffee shop).

Find what fires YOU up without exception and ignite that passion so that you routinely create YOUR Prizefighter day.

Acting with Courage and Integrity—Lieutenant J. Bobby Rehnquist

- Identify the truth and act from there with courage and integrity.
- TEAM WORK – Ego is I, Team is WE.
- Appreciate all people and the selfless acts and sacrifices they make daily.
- SEAL motto: *The only easy day was yesterday.*

Creating a Living Legacy—Dr. Rose Barnes

- Surrender to a cause greater than yourself.
- Create a *Living Legacy* and work diligently to fulfill it.
- Fight for what you believe in, regardless of the odds stacked up against you.

Living Legacy Exercise

Identify YOUR top five philosophers and philosophies that have impacted your life and will have an impact on your legacy. Each of us is writing the story of our lives, and at some point in time we will pass our pen to the next generation with lessons for them to leave for their legacies.

1. _____
2. _____
3. _____
4. _____

"Working through the remaining exercises together, you will take them back and inspire your teams. I propose we meet each morning, exploring how regular engagement of these techniques can define, hone, and strengthen your individual abilities and direction, and will ultimately define, hone, and strengthen our company." A flicker of annoyance registered around the room. Nobody wanted to do this now, nor this week; yet nobody had the courage to speak up. Even if they were now considered to be on equal footing with Pierce, they all knew this was only in theory. In reality, Pierce remained the owner and the boss, and the boss's mind appeared to be made up. The best they could all do was go along with it.

As the new board of directors filed down the hallway like a herd of cattle, Anderson overheard Hugo whispering to Ethan Williams, "Believe in the greatness of WE? Doesn't he mean, believe in the greatness of ME?" In this moment, he knew his greatest task would be keeping the entire leadership team on track and keeping Pierce well out of their way until the merger was complete. Pierce had been feared by many prior to his journey, and now it was clear they were beginning to despise him—a dangerous predicament for BlackBird Tech. This was also a dangerous predicament for Anderson and the entire board of directors . . . if they wanted to keep their jobs.

5

Chaos

Whether you believe you can
or you can't, you are right.
—Henry Ford

BlackBird Tech's newly appointed board of directors obsequiously showed up at 9:30 each morning that week, learning and participating in techniques that admittedly contained merit, if only the timing had been right. Nobody could argue that the exercises did not fire them up, dare them to think outside of the box, or inspire them to aim higher, yet they all felt they were under far too much pressure to meet the merger deadline while simultaneously easing the restructuring of their respective divisions into place. Protests had fallen on deaf ears. Fired up and excited by the prospect of sharing the pearls of wisdom gleaned from his inspirational journey, Pierce remained blind to fact that his entire board of directors—being pulled in all directions—was exhausted and stressed.

As the weeks rolled on, the merger inched closer, and one by one the team leaders each paid a visit to the one man they could count on to listen: Anderson Phillips. Most complained that they were at the office by 6:30 each morning in order to regain the sixty to ninety minutes Pierce took up at 9:30. Some stayed on well into the evening to complete their own work-load, having invested their days in redefining the roles of individuals under their leadership while reassuring them that they would retain their jobs, salaries, 401(k), and insurance. People had become nervous and uncertain, which resulted in them being unfocused and unproductive. Rumors rippled throughout the entire company that layoffs were coming—fueled by the imminent merger and notion of cheap labor in India—and many spent their company time polishing resumes and scouring the Internet and professional networks for employment opportunities. It all felt counterintuitive to the wisdom Pierce was aiming to teach.

"Did he hit his knee in that accident, or his head?"

"Excuse me?" Anderson looked up from his desk, shocked to see the usually quiet and composed J.P. red-faced and disheveled, pacing like a madman.

"Pierce! Is he out of his freaking mind? I can't tell anymore!" As J.P. collapsed into the soft gray chair in front of Anderson's desk, a greasy lock of hair flopped over the lens of his glasses. "Please tell me he hit his head in the accident—it will all make a hell of a lot more sense if you do."

"You know, I think he did hit his head, but apparently there was no damage." Anderson smiled encouragingly, "Tell me what's going on."

"What's going on?" J.P. leaned forward in his seat, eyebrows furrowing into a sharp "V" above his wire-framed eyewear. "What's going on? Are you kidding me? It's a shambles out there! Nobody knows if they are coming or going. Pierce waltzes in at 9:30 and is out by 3:00—and that would be fine if he left it at that, but he calls at all hours with random ideas, pulling manpower away from key projects."

"I'll talk to him."

"*Talk to him?* The man has intimidated every poor soul that has punched the clock for years; he ignites the fear of God in our people. They are jumping on board with whatever requirement he makes for fear of losing their jobs if they resist."

"Has he threatened this?" A sour bile rose from Anderson's stomach to his throat.

"No, no . . . of course not; you've seen him! He's like Polly-freaking-Anna flitting around—a whirlwind of positivity and smiles. And that's the problem, he *THINKS* he is doing the right thing—building on this ideal of a team working on equal ground, each division seamlessly merging and supporting one another as the divisiveness of hierarchy simply melts away. Change is never that straightforward and simple. We are all working our asses off in an attempt to make it magically happen for him, and he's directly calling key people and yanking them away from vital, time-sensitive projects, giving them little jobs to take care of."

Anderson felt angered and intrigued. He was well aware that the pressure of restructuring at an inconvenient time was straining their key people, but he had no idea Pierce had been undermining their best efforts. "What do you mean, 'little jobs'?"

J.P. removed his glasses, rubbed his bloodshot eyes, and sighed resignedly. "Anderson, I am sorry to be dumping this on you . . . but I am afraid we are beginning to look like a bunch of amateurs to our Indian counterparts at Nabhas, and our friends in New Delhi are getting cold feet. I heard through the grapevine they are revisiting an acquisition offer made by Boeing long before we were in the picture." J.P. ran his hands through his thinning hair and carefully replaced his glasses. Straightening in his chair, he looked Anderson directly in the eye. "BlackBird Tech was attractive to Nabhas because the owners would retain a percentage of stock in the company once it merged. Boeing wanted to buy them outright, but the passive earning potential of a BlackBird/Nabhas merger, long term, was far more attractive than the Boeing offer . . . until we began to unravel.

"And now the Boeing offer seems more attractive, given the security of a flat-out acquisition by a stable, well-run company . . . I get it.

"I know Pierce means well. He worked hard to build this company; there is no way he would self-destruct . . . which made me, you know, ask about his head."

Anderson smiled. "I hear you. I've heard a lot of things, actually, but I believed the issues were largely internal and something we would eventually gain a handle on. Now that you've brought Boeing to my attention, the need to act swiftly is glaringly obvious . . . I think it is time to have a courageous conversation with our commander."

J.P. sank back, surrendering to the chair. "Thank you."

"In the meantime, J.P., call the board together and order them to withdraw from any distractions Pierce has created. Draw up a direct plan to get Nabhas back on track immediately. Nobody is to work on anything else until the deal is done. Nobody."

J.P. leaned forward in his seat, "Anderson, they're afraid of him . . . he *is* the big kahuna."

"We're an equal team now, remember? Yet, as co-chair of the board, I am going to pull rank and make a company-wide order effective immediately. Nobody is to take direction from Pierce until they hear otherwise either directly from you or me."

"People are fearful for their jobs, their livelihood," said J.P.

"And they'll be protected."

"Can you guarantee that?"

"No, but it is the only way we are going to save this deal. Now, if you'll excuse me, I want to gather my facts together before I track Pierce down."

6

Resisting the Truth

*What lies before us and what lies
behind us are tiny matters compared
to what lies within us.*
—Ralph Waldo Emerson

"Anderson!" Pierce genuinely lit up when his former VP entered the quiet sanctuary of his book-lined office shortly after lunch. Carefully placing his pen on his desk, he gestured for Anderson to have a seat in the adjacent chair.

Deliberately lowering himself into the stiff brown leather, Anderson drew a slow and steady breath to center himself. Calling it a courageous conversation had not been far from the truth; he felt he needed the strength of a lion to confront his boss, a man well known to be impulsive and highly reactive. Anderson took his time, choosing his words and approach carefully.

"Thank you for meeting with me on such short notice."

"Hey, no problem!" Pierce certainly was upbeat, like he popped a happy pill for lunch. Anderson smiled, recollecting J.P.'s Pollyanna comment.

"Pierce, we're having some communication problems within the organization that I was hoping you could help me resolve."

"Sure, what seems to be the problem?"

Anderson drew another slow, steady breath and let out a sigh before cautiously presenting his case. "Well, for a start, there is a lot of confusion regarding role definition and project delegation."

"Anderson, we no longer *have* distinct roles, but *TEAMS*, in place, eliminating the need for role definition and project delegation. Our teams work in unison to complete projects—there is no delegation beyond deciding which team is best qualified for each project. "

"Nobody knows exactly what that means, Pierce. Theoretically, the concept is understood. But, as *I* understand it, YOU have been drawing individuals away from their teams to work on individual projects, undermining the whole team concept you are subscribing to." Pierce flushed, taken aback by this apparent attack from his second in charge. Who did Anderson think he was, accusing him of undermining his own employees?

Pushing his chair out from under him, Pierce hobble-paced, cursing under his breath at the pain in his knee. He needed to move quickly, knowing he could not sustain himself sitting in the hot seat facing Anderson without exploding. Desperately trying to conjure some of Jon's calmness, he flailed about the office, finally settling in a stance looking out the window. He defiantly stuffed his hands deep within his trouser pockets, turned his back to Anderson, and shifted the weight to his good leg.

"I can assure you, Anderson, I have BlackBird Tech's best interests at heart. And I have not been undermining anyone."

Glancing at notes made prior to this meeting, Anderson began to make his point. "Anuj was working through the final stages integrating software systems for BlackBird and Nabhas. In fact, it was almost complete by the due date two weeks ago—that is, until you called him at 4:00 one afternoon and set forth the task of developing seamless luggage retrieval systems for commercial passengers!" Anderson strained to mask the incredulity in his voice.

"One extra job? What kind of people do we have working for us if they cannot complete several tasks? As a team, they have the leverage to be much more productive."

"Pierce, it is not a question of teamwork. It is a question of focus. You're leading team members astray."

"Rubbish!" Pierce spat.

"Jane Evans?" Anderson cautiously brought up the sustainability leader's name.

"What about her?" Pierce fumed.

"She has been looking at Europe for inspiration on ways to 'green up' the company."

"We plan on doing business in Europe once we become BlackBird-Nabhas Global; we need to be green if we want to appeal to that market. The Europeans practically invented the whole green movement!"

"I agree, but right now, we need all hands on deck—focused on the current merger."

"Jane can handle it."

"Take the time to think this through and approach it differently. Or you're going to lose it all."

"What does that mean?"

"It means, we have heard from a very reliable source that Nabhas is getting cold on the deal."

"That's impossible, it's a done deal." Pierce resented baseless threats. He should never have allowed Anderson to run the company in his absence. Foolishly misguided, he had grossly misjudged Anderson's capabilities, personality, and ego; apparently the power had gone to his head after all.

"It *was* a done deal when we were a highly functioning company; right now we are chaotic and amateurish at best. We've not delivered what was required of us in a timely manner because nobody knows what they are supposed to be doing. Nabhas has every right to withdraw." Pierce stared out the window as Anderson, softening his tone, drove the final nail in.

"Teamwork is WE, ego is I . . . There is no team here, buddy, only a group of fearful, unsettled people anxious about their job security. I have been hearing from them all week; nobody knows, or understands, his or her place anymore—nor what they are supposed to be working on. You preach working smarter, yet most of your team leaders are burning the candle at both ends. They are working longer hours than ever before and scrambling to meet your suggestions for change while simultaneously working—*scrambling*—to save the deal." Pierce bristled. Had his plans really derailed so badly? With all of his effort to the contrary, it seemed impossible.

"I've made it *easy* for everyone! Without *my* willingness to implement change, they'd all be stuck behind their desks getting ordered around. By personally empowering each and every employee I stripped away the hierarchy pyramid. They should be grateful, not bitching behind my back to you because I threw them a bone and gave them one or two new innovative projects to develop!"

"And your project suggestions are great and valid. They are innovative and will be brilliant developments in the future. Your timing, however, is wrong."

"Anuj could have spoken up if he had other priorities."

"Pierce, they're afraid of you."

Pierce was stung. *Afraid? Of him?* "Ludicrous!" He spat. "They're no more afraid of me than they are of Sabina!"

"Pierce, nobody knows who they are supposed to be answering to anymore. The lines are blurred, and they answer to anyone and everyone. And they especially answer to you. It is a complicated mess."

"I made myself and my vision CLEAR. Team leaders are in place to LEAD. If these morons messed it up and failed to lead properly, how is it *my* fault?" Pierce boomed.

"Pierce! Reframe!" Anderson—who rarely raised his voice—barked, taking both men by surprise.

"What, did you just say . . . refrain?"

"Reframe. I said reframe." Anderson's voice grew quiet and tired. He knew he was skating on thin ice, confronting his boss with the cold hard truth and, even worse, solid advice. Softening his tone, he rephrased his request, "It's time to examine and reframe your thinking."

Turning from the window, Pierce looked at Anderson as if for the first time. Suddenly Anderson morphed into all of the people he met on his journey; Jon, Bobby, Coach E., and Dr. Barnes stared back at him. "Reframe." He carefully rolled the word around in his mouth like an exotic fruit being tasted for the first time, uncertain of its edibility. "Reframe," he carefully repeated the word once again, this time with a little more certainty that the fruit was not poisonous and was, in fact, quite tasty.

Anderson looked on cautiously, an expert bullfighter calculating his beastly opponent's next move.

"Reframe." Pierce walked toward the chesterfield sofa. "Examine and reframe your thinking." Dropping onto the burgundy leather with a squeak, he added, "I like it."

Anderson had no idea where he pulled the phrase from—sure, he was familiar with the term and knew where he had learned the technique—yet he unintentionally blurted it out in a moment of frustration . . . and it had worked like a charm. While he could not be certain that Pierce really would change his thinking, the power of this one word or idea had stopped him in his tracks, shifting his mood from defensive and angry to curious and pensive in an instant.

Pierce sat quietly for a few moments as Anderson watched him, uncertain which side of Pierce's personality would resurface. Slowly lifting his gaze to meet Anderson's, Pierce asked earnestly, "I've been an ass again, haven't I?" Holding a palm in the air he added, "Rhetorical question, no need to answer."

Anderson was relieved Pierce had finally come to his senses. "Not entirely, your intentions and ideas for change are good—great even! Change doesn't happen overnight, not good change or change that sticks. It must be incremental, intentional, and authentic. And the timing needs to be right too . . ." he trailed off, not wanting to anger Pierce by hinting the pointless and childish retort, *I told you so.*

Pierce nodded. Anderson was right. The changes Pierce made so far had been as superficial as his big house—grandiose, sweeping changes that were all smoke and mirrors, manufactured to hide the fact he had failed to complete the necessary interior work to truly implement change. Pierce understood that he had not changed at all, merely "rearranged" things to appear that he had. Exhaling, he flopped back onto the sofa, surrendering to the realization he had not returned from a life-altering journey several weeks ago at all. Pierce Edwards's life-altering journey had only just begun.

7

Facing the Truth

*You can't always choose the path you walk
in life, but you can always choose the
manner in which you walk it.*
—John O'Leary

"Dr. Joseph Jasarevic, a sport psychologist, his practice is not even five minutes from here, in Charlotte Plaza."

"I had no idea you played sports." Pierce was intrigued; admittedly, he knew very little about Anderson Phillips.

"My son plays for Furman—point guard, full scholarship." Anderson beamed proudly. "Dr. Jasarevic helped him out when he was struggling with interpersonal issues, learning to balance and cope with studies *and* a grueling training schedule as a freshman."

"And the reframe exercise . . ." Pierce was becoming a huge fan of these simple and accessible techniques.

"Something we both learned in one of Paul's sessions. It helped Paul a lot. It showed him how to deal with frustrations and stopped him in his tracks whenever he felt overwhelmed. This technique encouraged him to think through each thought and subsequent action and identify a better response or more positive solution."

"So, this Dr. . . . Jasvic?"

"Jasarevic. Everybody calls him Dr. J."

"This Dr. J. books patients who are nonathletes?"

"I'm not certain. I can pull up his information for you if you like," Anderson offered.

"Sure, that would be great."

Both men remained quiet, well aware of the thick air swelling around them, heavy and pregnant with Pierce's unspoken apology. An apology he knew he should address. "Anderson, may I ask? Just how bad is it? The merger, is it *salvageable*?"

"Salvageable? I'm not sure." Anderson had to be honest. "This morning I met with J.P. and took the liberty of pulling everybody off any project unrelated to Nabhas. Working around the clock, I am hoping we can pull our act together and prove we are ready to merge and grow exponentially as a global empire. Our biggest problem is, Boeing is back in the picture and they're a strong contender. Our saving grace is that Boeing is still talking buyout. The founding partners at Nabhas were initially attracted to BlackBird based on our offer of perpetual equity."

"Scrambling to meet the merger requirements won't cut it. Do we need to offer them more equity?" Pierce was thinking out loud, he knew the minute the words crossed his lips this was not a viable route.

"We need them to believe in us once again." Anderson reaffirmed that throwing more money at prospective buyers would make them no more attractive, not without being a finely oiled and fully functioning machine.

"We need manpower lining up new accounts, proving we will be ready to grow exponentially immediately following the merger."

"Exactly."

"Who do you have on it?"

"J.P. put Tim Pope on it. He already had several leads building relationships in Britain—which would be the largest and most attractive new government contract we could possibly acquire. Several of his team members are looking into the smaller fish— military contracts in western European countries."

"Tim Pope. I haven't seen him at any of our team-leader meetings the past few weeks." Pierce had failed to notice the absence of the director of sales prior to this conversation.

Anderson cleared his throat, uncertain of how Pierce would receive the information he was about to share. "Tim has been on unpaid leave for the past three weeks; he returned to work yesterday."

Pierce cocked an eyebrow, surprised to be learning this for the first time.

"His wife was in a car accident and needed an emergency C-section to save the lives of their twin baby girls. Thank goodness all three of them survived. The twins were eight weeks premature—they're still in the neonatal unit, but Tim's wife was discharged several days ago and is doing well. I offered unpaid leave for as long as he needed to support his family. Sarah Jones stepped in and ran the division for him during his absence."

Pierce nodded solemnly. Anderson was impressive. Pierce knew if he been at the helm when the accident happened, he would never have allowed Tim indefinite leave. Even owed vacation and sick days would have been a stretch for him to approve at the dawn of a large deal. Dr. Rose Barnes and the question she had posed to him on his visit to her dingy little office in the back halls of the Boston Medical Center, weeks prior, came to mind: *Do you ever think about the hardships that individuals may be experiencing in their lives while they work for you? Or do you think only in terms of your profit and success?* It was clear to him that Anderson *did* think about the big picture—he cared about the individuals as much as he cared about the success of the company itself. Shamefully, Pierce had no idea Tim Pope and his wife were expecting. Appallingly, Tim had almost lost his entire family, and Pierce was only learning about it today.

Anderson was clearly qualified to run BlackBird Tech *and* direct the merger successfully. Pierce knew it was time to truly step down and trust the people he appointed as leaders to do just that—lead. For the first time, he was beginning to grasp that what he had learned on his journey—the deep, profound wisdom four successful people had generously shared with him—was so much more than simple techniques and exercises to practice each morning in hopes of magically transforming his life. He needed to roll his sleeves up and *work* toward change. These exercises and techniques were valuable tools to keep him on track and he would continue to engage in them every day, but they had to be complemented by some good old-fashioned, nitty-gritty hard work. He hoped he had found a mentor to guide him on this journey in Dr. J.—if he had the goodness in his heart to agree to take on a nonathlete, pompous businessman as a client.

"Anderson, it sounds like you have it under control. I said I was stepping down as CEO a few weeks ago, yet I failed to follow through on that. I apologize for any extra work, chaos, or frustration my actions have created. You're a valuable asset to the company, and I want you at the helm, leading the merger and leading the new BlackBird Tech when the merger is completed. I do expect to be kept up to date, but from now on, major and minor decisions will be in your capable hands. If you don't mind, I would like to announce and confirm these changes at our team meeting tomorrow."

"Sounds fair. Thank you, Pierce." Anderson was too relieved to be pleased with what sounded suspiciously like a permanent promotion.

"One last thing, before you leave today."

"Sure."

"Send me Dr. J.'s contact information. I have a good feeling he can help me sort through some of my . . . er, control issues." Pierce smiled hopefully at his new commander.

"You got it."

8

Changing Habits, Changing THINKING

YOUR success is not just about changing YOUR habits; it's about changing the way YOU think.

Sitting in Dr. J.'s contemporary waiting area, Pierce nervously flicked through dated copies of *Esquire* and *Sports Illustrated*. It was 8:30 a.m. on a Wednesday and the first day in three weeks that he had not dropped the kids off at school. Amazing how quickly something could feel so routine that a palpable void was evident once the routine altered. Sarah must have missed it too; she seemed a little lost in the mornings ushering Pierce and the kids to the Escalade in her robe, uncertain of what to do next as they waved their goodbyes; she quite literally jumped at the opportunity to take the kids when he had asked her last night. Habit was a funny thing, challenging to create but, once formed, equally if not *doubly* challenging to let go. At this precise moment in his thinking, Pierce looked up and noticed a small framed sign on Dr. J.'s wall: *YOUR success is not just about changing YOUR habits; it's about changing the way YOU think*. Pierce felt he had come to the right place indeed.

The glass door to Dr. J.'s office opened and a tall, thin man in his early fifties appeared. Of eastern-European descent, Dr. J. had striking blue-gray eyes, a broad clean-shaven face, and unusually high cheekbones that made him look like he was permanently smiling. As Dr. J. gripped his hand in a firm, warm handshake, Pierce knew he was going to enjoy working with the kind-spirited psychologist who had agreed to step out of his usual circle of clientele for a friend of a friend—Anderson Phillips.

It turned out Anderson's son had been a patient for only a brief time as a freshman, yet Anderson remained good friends with the doctor, who had attended all of Furman's home games as a guest of Anderson and his wife, Molly. One call from Anderson, and Pierce was penciled in to see Dr. J. the following morning. Admittedly, it was the kind of service Pierce expected, yet he never had to rely on somebody else in order to get it.

Gesturing for Pierce to take a seat on a rather comfortable yet extremely minimalist European-style sofa, Dr. J. strolled to a small kitchenette at the far side of his office. "Tea?" he offered.

"That would be great; thank you."

"Green okay?"

"Whatever you have."

Pierce was surprised when Dr. J. took a seat right next to him on the sofa after carefully setting an elegant teapot on the table. Uncertain as to why this apparent snub of conventionalism unsettled him, it felt strangely intimate and almost unprofessional. Pierce expected a *doctor*—complete with leather psychiatrist's chaise and clipboard filled with standardized questions that he would ask in a monotone voice, peering over wire-rimmed glasses from a stiff chair *on the other side of the room*! He did not expect to be sitting side-by-side on a tidy European sofa sipping tea like old friends. But that was exactly Dr. J.'s tactic and the reason he was so successful.

Wrapping his hands around the cup, the habit of closing his eyes, soaking up the aroma, and dropping into the moment did not fail Pierce, and he immediately began to relax. Dr. J. watched closely, a knowing smile spreading across his face. Opening his eyes, Pierce smiled goofily and explained, "Habit."

"I see." Dr. J. responded before quietly picking up his cup and sipping his own tea.

Silence.

"Anderson speaks very highly of you," Pierce offered, desperate to get a conversation rolling.

Dr. J. nodded, replacing the cup on its delicate saucer. "He is a good man, Anderson. Ever seen his son Paul play? Amazing basketball player, and bright, bright kid—huge future . . . nice family."

Pierce smiled and nodded, what could he possibly say. He had only met Anderson's wife a handful of times at holiday parties over the years and had no idea they even had a son until yesterday. Dr. J. most likely had a fairly accurate idea of what a knucklehead Pierce had been, yet he decided not to incriminate himself from the start and pretended to agree with the doctor's assessment of the Phillips clan.

"Very nice family." Pierce affirmed with a smile.

"And what brings you to my office on this fine fall morning, Pierce?"

Relieved to be getting down to business, Pierce sat forward in his seat to tell Dr. J. his story. Dr. J. listened carefully, not once interrupting the rhetoric as Pierce relayed the story of Sarah and Josh's intervention. He shared how reluctant he was to embark on the journey set forth by his wife and best friend, considering his old work habits and beliefs. He then told Dr. J. of his impassioned return—how he was suddenly revved up and inspired by an overwhelming drive to make big changes in his work and personal life. He went on to describe the four people he encountered on his journey and the valuable lessons each had imparted. And then, he told this stranger with the friendly face—who, by daring to sit right next to him, was beginning to feel like an old and trusted friend—his most shameful secret. Despite his desperate bid to change and the greatest of efforts, he had almost lost it all. Pierce Edwards had come precariously close to failure.

After a moment of silence Dr. J. rubbed his chin dramatically. "I see." A long beat passed before he spoke again, summarizing what Pierce had told him. "So you went at it like a bull in a china shop. Could not see the forest for the trees!" Flopping his hand around he added, "Yada, yada, yada . . . insert any quaint old colloquialism of your choice to justify what is perfectly normal human behavior."

Pierce was stung. He expected Dr. J. to come up with something better than that. His own grandmother would have offered a similar superstitious summary; he expected a heck of a lot more insight from professional psychologist of Dr. J.'s caliber.

"Pierce, it seems you were inspired enough to want to make some pretty sweeping changes to your home and work life. And this is a very important step, imperative in fact; you need to *want* to change in order to do so. Don't you agree?"

Pierce nodded in agreement. "Of course."

"What I am hearing when you talk is a fairly common pitfall most people embarking on change experience." Pierce hung on Dr. J.'s every word.

"Most people, Pierce, change their habits from the outside;

they start working less, or commit to going to the gym every day, or change their diet . . . whatever it is they are trying to change, they do so by *removing* what they don't want to be or identify with, and believe they are done. They believe this gesture alone will be enough. WANTING to change—that overwhelming desire to change that drives you to improve, whether it be for your wife, your best friend, your family, your company, or for YOURSELF—is the most important step. The second most important step is less about making the actual changes—this will occur organically—it is about changing the way YOU *THINK!*"

Dr. J. allowed Pierce to ruminate on his words, letting a few moments pass before adding, "It is the only way one can truly implement change, Pierce, recalibrating the way one thinks and allowing change to grow from a space of genuine belief and truth. It is also the hardest and most challenging step and the reason so many people fail."

"I've heard about your REFRAME exercise from Anderson. Is this how you learn to think differently? Playing gatekeeper to my thoughts, do I 'reframe' each time I recognize a moment when I need to think differently?" Pierce asked.

Dr. J. laughed heartily, "If only it were that simple, Pierce! In short, you are correct; this is certainly something we will work on. But before we begin to work on your thinking, we need to explore the why. *Why* do you want to change? What are your motives? What is your inspiration? What do you hope to achieve?"

Pierce did not know where to begin! He knew his story, the one he had just relayed in its entirety to Dr. J., yet he did not know how to answer these questions coherently . . . or truthfully. *Why do I want to change?* he wondered to himself.

Because I have been an ass, my wife wants me to, I want to be a better father and husband, I don't want to work myself to an early grave, or *because I want to be liked and respected?* No specific reason stood out. Did it have to? He did not know. He struggled with the remaining questions Dr. J. had posed . . . not landing on anything with real clarity.

"Allow me to offer you some direction." Pierce was relieved when Dr. J. broke the silence. "These four people you met on your journey, who you say really inspired you. I want you to think about each one of them. Take your time and really think about each individual. Then tell me what these individuals had in common."

Pierce thought for a long time about each of his mentors, connecting the dots to characteristics and traits they all shared. Dr. J. slid a notepad and pen to Pierce, "This may help you."

The doctor busied himself with making more tea as Pierce scribbled on the notepad. Pierce stopped to think momentarily before striking a comment out or drawing a solid line connecting two thoughts. After a good fifteen minutes passed, Pierce placed the pen down; he had completed his task.

"Well, how did you do?" Dr. J. asked good-naturedly.

Reaching for the notepad, Pierce shrugged uncertainly.

"Well, let's hear it."

Sighing heavily, Pierce read aloud from his list, "Fitness and energy levels—despite their age—was the first common denominator I noticed."

"Very good, go on."

"Breathing and centering techniques—they all either demonstrated or mentioned the value in practicing such techniques, this would be the second. I listed five," Pierce offered.

"Great! Go on." Dr. J. smiled encouragingly.

"Thinking before they speak, being impeccable with their words, or speaking the truth. Next I noticed that they all possess big-picture thinking—or seeing the trees *and* the forest." He smiled at Dr. J., who laughed.

"Finally, they all take pride in building a team, sharing the work *and* the credit for their success, and trusting and believing in the teams they built."

"Very good. Excellent. This is a great start. The traits you recognize in those who inspire you, and more importantly, the common traits linking them all, are what inspire you the most. Call it mirroring, if you will. Individual characteristics and beliefs can and will provide inspiration, too. But, the common traits are most impactful and easiest to implement."

"And now the big question to ask yourself, Pierce, is which— if any—of these traits do you believe you already possess, could easily implement, or may have trouble implementing?"

Pierce sighed heavily. He thought he *was* on track to make changes with great progress. Yet, it turned out that he was not, and it almost cost him the biggest deal his company had negotiated—and it still could. That's what had brought him to Dr. J. in the first place. He needed to REFRAME, as Anderson had pointed out, but he had no idea where or how he skidded so spectacularly off the rails to begin with. As simple as the whole reframing technique sounded, he had no idea where to redirect his thinking. Wasn't he doing everything he could already? What more could he possibly do?

"I don't know the answer to that, in all honesty," He looked at Dr. J. for a long moment before adding, "I thought I *was* on track, implementing the ideals of those who inspire me most. But I guess somehow my desire to implement these changes was hampered by my ability to do so."

Dr. J. smiled, "There's a famous Wooden quote—you mentioned your guy from St. Louis, the coach who played for and was profoundly inspired by Wooden himself."

Pierce nodded.

"Ability is a poor man's wealth."

Pierce's nostrils flared indignant, "I am NOT poor!" He shouted defensively.

"Well then, you have not only the ability, but the means to truly impact your life, the lives of those you love, and your community too. But do you have the desire?"

"Of course I do! That's why I am here!" Pierce remained on edge. He was absolutely fueled by desire and was angered that this renowned sport psychologist failed to see that. What kind of quack was this guy? Pierce's mind unraveled, swiftly and dramatically falling from the secure feeling that he had come to the right person for help to the clear fact that it had been a very big mistake coming to Dr. J. "I left my wife and children for eleven days, traveling the country—left my business right in the middle of an important merger negotiation—to find my truth and inspiration. I *changed* the entire structure of my company upon my return and worked daily on exercises given to me by my four mentors—I even introduced these to my coworkers to inspire change within them, and all for a *greater* purpose." Pierce threw his hands in the air in defeat. "If that's not desire, Dr. J., then please enlighten me, what is?"

Dr. J. leaned back on the sofa, a bemused expression on his face that pissed Pierce off even more—the fact that he was sitting so close *and* had the audacity to smirk at him! The nerve!

"Very well. The point I am making, Pierce, is that implementing change is where you failed—it is where most people fail, despite their best intentions. Changing your thinking is key and will be the essence of our work together. Fueled by great and genuine desire, this work is not about practicing a couple of techniques and then going on about your day. It requires commitment and it is damn hard. If you possess the ability *and* the desire—then you have the perfect ingredients for success if you apply yourself to the work. Are you willing to apply yourself to the work?"

"When do we begin?" Pierce asked defiantly.

"Tomorrow. In fact, if you can make the time, I would like to see you each morning at 8:00, starting tomorrow. Bring your mentor's techniques along . . . we will work through them together. And I have a few of my own techniques to introduce when the time is right." He smiled warmly at Pierce, who still felt oddly defiant. Dr. J. had challenged him somewhat, and Pierce felt fired up to meet the challenge.

* * *

Sarah beamed at her husband when he sheepishly confessed that he could no longer keep up with dropping the kids at school—but he promised, *promised*, he would pick them up each and every afternoon. Bored out of her mind most mornings, she felt a rush of relief that her familial responsibilities were being returned to her, and she could not be happier. Yet a bubble of concern arose, a black smudge marring her golden mood. Was Pierce backtracking? Slipping, one step at a time, back to his former self? Would he next be saying he could no longer collect the kids in the afternoon or that he would have to skip soccer practice, then parent-teacher night? Work late through family dinners? Drink? Sarah shook herself back to reality with a jolt—she would not allow such thinking—her role was to support Pierce, not imagine his demise.

Because Pierce failed to keep Sarah apprised of the debacle at work, she was clueless as to why he felt the need to work so tirelessly with his new mentor, this Dr. J. character. Pierce had changed dramatically, there was no doubt in her mind about that. Perhaps this was his way of making sure he stayed on track for her and the kids. She shrugged off lingering fears and allowed pride to swell within her. Snuggling closer to her husband, she watched the sunset over the rolling hills behind their property as Lila and Max chased each other through the garden. Sarah had never felt so content as she did in that precise moment. A moment abruptly shattered by the ringing of Pierce's cell phone.

Pierce listened for a long moment as Anderson relayed the status of the Nabhas deal to him. Sarah eyed Pierce as he paced back and forth along the length of the patio. Finally it was Pierce who spoke, "Sounds like you have it under control. No, no, I don't think there is any need for me to be there, you go ahead and lead the meeting. I will be in just after ten o'clock or so. If you need me before, call my cell." Pierce smiled, looking over at Sarah swinging on the loveseat, he added, "Another journey? Yes, you could say that, but this time no further than Dr. J.'s office." Hanging up, he hobbled back to join Sarah on the loveseat. They swung silently for several minutes before he leaned in, took her face in both hands and said, "Thank you." Sarah responded with a smile, her heart overflowing with love and hope.

9

Review, Reframe, Renew: Sessions with Dr. J.

Blessed is the man who perseveres under trial, for when he has stood the test, he will receive the crown of life that God has promised to those who love him.

—James 1:12 NIV

Session #1
Thursday, November 13, 2014
8:00 a.m.

Dr. J. carefully flipped through the little booklet of exercises Pierce brought along to the session—the same collection Sabina had compiled for the staff on his first morning back at the office. Now seated—still rather uncomfortably—*next to* this renowned sport psychologist, Pierce mentally prepared himself to take the final imperative steps toward true change. Work.

"Very, very good." Dr. J. smiled at Pierce and placed the papers on the table in front of them. "How often did you implement these techniques?"

"Daily," Pierce affirmed with a sense of pride.

"Humph . . . Very, very good." Dr. J. repeated his sentiment.

A long moment passed before Dr. J. slid a notepad in front of Pierce. "Let's start at the beginning. How does that sound, Pierce?" Pierce shrugged; where else would they start? "We will work with two exercises today; one of them is yours, and I would like to introduce one of mine. Let's begin with yours."

Peering over his glasses, Dr. J. squinted at the pages Pierce had given him. "*Attaining Belief in Yourself.* Take out a piece of paper," he said, tapping his knuckles on the notepad in front of Pierce, "and write down an idea about the person you want to be and the life you want to live."

The defensive feeling from the previous day arose once again in Pierce. This was a complete waste of time, he had already done this exercise, and he resented Dr. J. for dragging him through the murky waters of redundancy. Sensing resistance, Dr. J. stopped Pierce. "Read through the 'Key Factors' of this exercise with me for a moment, Pierce. Number one, *ACCEPT the TRUTH*. You would not be seated here with me today had you not acknowledged and accepted the simple truth that you desired change. What is that change, Pierce; who do you want to be?"

"Well, I—" Dr. J. raised a hand to silence him.

"Rhetorical question. Let's move through these together to gain clarity. Then I want you to work through them at your own pace on your own time." As Dr. J. charged a rate of $500 per hour, this was music to Pierce's ears. "*SPEAK the TRUTH*—a tough but necessary step. It is not about who you want to be, but who you *do not* want to be. It is the part of you that you do not want to identify with—the very part you need to shine a bright spotlight on. Habits, regrets—list them all and we will discuss them together . . . understand?"

Pierce nodded obsequiously. Nothing was going to get past Dr. J. Though Pierce had only barely scratched the surface in regards to working with him, he already felt stark naked. "*BREATHE through the TRUTH*—my understanding of this is that you will not judge or beat yourself up over any-thing that arises from the previous step . . . We are panning for gold, and any seasoned gold miner will tell you that you must to pan through a lot of shit to find the tiniest speck of gold." Pierce was startled by this proper gentleman's use of a mild, yet crass, word. But his point was clearly understood. Pierce had approached the exercise with a completely different understanding when Jon originally passed it along to him. All sunshine, lollipops, and rainbows, he optimistically looked forward to who he wanted to be and barely skimmed reflection, viewing it as a frivolous waste of time. Uninterested in who he *was*, Pierce was on the fast track to get to who he thought he should be, and Dr. J. was not going to allow him to make the same mistake twice.

"*PROCESS the TRUTH*—gain a full understanding of who you are and who you want to be, and explore what steps you need to take in order to bridge the gap. *CREATE a plan based on the TRUTH*—again, this is not so much about who you want to be, but who you are now and what you need to change in order to get where you want to be."

"I did make changes and I already do believe in myself—can't we just skip this exercise?" The whiny tone in his own voice surprised Pierce.

"Pierce, you admitted to me in our previous session that you felt the changes you made were superficial. You failed to complete the nitty-gritty work—like most people when they embark on similar endeavors. You cannot jump to who you want to be—cannot change your THINKING to who you want to be—without taking a good hard look at who you are."

"A pompous jerk." Pierce offered.

"Fair enough, but I think you were much more than that—you were a successful businessman, a husband, and a father. How you viewed yourself in these roles drove you to make the choices and decisions you made each and every moment of your life up to this point. How do you want to view yourself in these roles in the future? This is a very good exercise that your friend gave you, Pierce; it is gold. If you don't mind, I would like to keep a copy to use with some of my other clients—this is a crucial stepping-stone in the process."

"Okay, okay . . . I understand." Pierce knew he had to do the work, there was no way around it, as attractive as a short cut would be. The thought that he could pop a magic pill and all would be changed was mere fantasy. Why was he always in a hurry? Always after a quick fix to get the results he wanted? Coach E. had talked about focusing on the process and not the results—and now Dr. J. was, in his own way, saying the same thing; but damn, it was much easier said than done.

"I have a similar exercise that I also want you to complete. Safety in numbers," Dr. J. said, smiling broadly. "By covering all bases I am confident we will reveal the core of your truth much more quickly." Dr. J. passed another sheet of paper to Pierce to study.

YOUR Legacy Statement

Purpose Statement: _____

_____

_____

Who are YOU??? (YOUR 'I AM' Statements): _____

_____

_____

1-year vision and 5-year vision: _____

_____

_____

What is the TRUE MEASURE of YOUR Success: _____

_____

_____

Who are YOU??? (YOUR 'I AM' Statements): _____

_____

_____

"Questions?" Dr. J. responded to Pierce's puzzled expression.

"Tons." Pierce smiled back at Dr. J., hoping he could shine some clarity on something that had bugged him ever since meeting Dr. Rose Barnes in Boston. "Legacy. What is it to you, Dr. J.? You call this *YOUR Legacy Statement,* and I was given an exercise by my fourth mentor, Dr. Barnes, that was all about *Creating a LIVING Legacy.* There appears to be a gravitational pull toward legacy, yet I am not one hundred percent convinced I know exactly what it is. I thought I did, but now I only feel confused by the notion of legacy—particularly focusing on it while living."

Dr. J. leaned forward, much to Pierce's dismay, and scratched the word "Legacy" from the paper; in one swift move it went from "YOUR Legacy Statement" to simply "YOUR Statement."

"Legacy is about YOU, Pierce, it is about who you are and what impact you make on your community as that person. We will absolutely get to this point, but for now I want to focus on crawling before we break into a full-blown legacy sprint. First, let's get to the root of who you are and who you want to be. Clear definition will lay the solid foundation that can guide you to identify what legacy means to you." Glancing furtively at his watch, Dr. J. politely wrapped the session, sending Pierce away to diligently complete his homework. Two exercises: Attaining Belief in Yourself and YOUR Legacy Statement.

Strolling toward the nearest Starbucks to begin his inner exploration, Pierce felt like a high school student readying himself for college once again. Perched on the cusp of the unknown, a giddy mix of exhilaration and trepidation colored his being.

Session #2
Friday, November 14, 2014
8:00 a.m.

Disheveled and tired, Pierce lounged on Dr. J.'s fine European sofa, his feet resting on the low coffee table in front of him. If this act of defiance and disregard for Dr. J.'s furniture bothered Dr. J., he did not show it. Quietly humming a nondescript tune, he carefully read through all of Pierce's notes. It took him about fifteen minutes. Placing the notes on the table next to Pierce's size-twelve boots, he then busied himself making yet another pot of tea. Pierce wondered how much tea the doctor went through in a week—it was barely 8:20 a.m. and this was the second pot Pierce had witnessed brewing. With fondness he thought of Jon and his obsession with tea, making a mental note to reach out to him this weekend to see how he was doing.

Repositioning himself alongside Pierce, Dr. J. finally broke the silence. "Excellent work, Pierce."

"But I didn't finish it—" Pierce fumbled his words. His frustration became apparent, lacing his deep voice with whine. "The 'I AM' statement . . ." he trailed off, not quite knowing where to go. He had spent the better part of the previous day struggling with this part of the exercise. Jon's technique, *Attaining Belief in Yourself,* had proven easier on its second run; approaching it once again with a strong notion of where he had failed before, Pierce succeeded in taking an honest and in-depth look at who he had been, rapidly chalking up the stark contrasts between who he was and who he wanted to be.

Creating a visual timeline, he scored extra brownie points for himself by mapping out the possible directions he could take in order to achieve his goals. The "I AM" statement was where he became completely and utterly stuck. He no longer identified with who he was—the desire to change coupled with the close examination of who he had been caused him to distance himself from the old version of Pierce. Not yet who he aspired to be, the work to get there had only just begun. To say "I AM," by Pierce's interpretation, could only refer to who he was in the moment, and he did not know the answer to that. He felt lost and a little confused—the present Pierce was in limbo, awkwardly dangling between two very different representations of himself. Pierce Edwards, who always had an answer for everything, was unquestionably stuck, and it unsettled him greatly.

Tossing and turning for most of the night, he finally rose at 5:00 a.m. and went for a long run around the neighborhood. His injured knee protested profusely, but he battled through the pain and resistance, knowing he would pay the price later. With running being the best way to clear his head, it seemed like a fair trade-off at the time. Distant with Sarah and the kids that morning, he sulked about in his home office trying to come up with an answer before his 8:00 a.m. appointment. An overachiever by nature, his inability to come up with a reasonable "I AM" statement left him feeling acutely disappointed and ashamed, as if he were an absolute failure.

"Pierce," Dr. J. spoke softly, as if a newborn he dare not awaken slept between them. "I intentionally introduced that exercise to you with very little direction to highlight the importance of changing your thinking. This is the key step in doing so." Exhausted from overthinking, the last thing Pierce wanted to think about was *changing* his thinking. He listened benignly to the doctor's explanation. "The purpose of your 'I AM' statement is to envision yourself right now, in this moment, as the person you want to be . . . understand?" Pierce politely nodded through the foggy haze of fatigue.

"Allow me to share a former client's story with you, a young NFL player named Wes Camden."

Pierce nodded robotically and sank back further into the lounge. Whether he agreed to it or not, he knew Dr. J. was going to tell the story, and he figured he might as well be comfortable.

"As a senior in college, Wes was captain of a Big Ten university team with aspirations of being drafted into the NFL as a linebacker. The scouts predicted him to run a 4.85 forty-yard dash at best, and Wes—as well as any scout worth his salt—knew this was not going to be enough to garner the attention

96

of the NFL. In fact, Wes knew his lifelong record for the forty-yard dash was 4.6, only slightly faster than the scouts' estimate. Wes had two choices." Dr. J. held up two fingers, folding one at a time as he made each point. "He could either give up on his dream of playing pro football, or he could fight for it.

"Training harder and pushing harder physically and mentally, he told himself from day one, *I AM a linebacker that runs a 4.59 forty-yard dash*. Over and over again he repeated this to himself, until it became him. The scout's 4.85 predictions did not exist, his 4.6 record did not exist; Wes Camden was a linebacker who ran a 4.59 forty-yard dash." Dr. J. strolled toward a bay of windows that overlooked College Street; standing with his hands nestled in his pockets, he looked down at the busy morning traffic and continued to relay his story.

"The regional pro day drew close and, unfortunately, Wes suffered a sports hernia during training, causing excruciating pain down his entire left side. Training so incredibly hard for this day, Wes had made a multitude of personal sacrifices. He trained his butt off physically *and* completed challenging internal psychological work to attain an unwavering belief in his ability; this injury, threatening his opportunity to fight for a spot in the NFL, seemed cruelly unfair.

"Sports hernia and all, Wes completed each stage of the pro day—showing NFL scouts exactly what he was made of, proving he would be a viable and valuable asset to a professional team. When it came time to toe up to the forty-yard dash line, the belief he was a linebacker that ran a 4.59 forty-yard dash resonated to his very core. However, Wes Camden did not run a 4.59 forty-yard dash that day. Though suffering with a hernia that riddled him with pain, he completed his dash in just 4.54 seconds, faster than he believed—*truly believed*—he was capable, rapidly and deservedly garnering the attention of NFL scouts."

Leaning against the bank of windows, Dr. J. allowed the sun to warm his back as he reveled in telling Wes Camden's story. Working with countless athletes over the years, he always maintained Wes's to be one of the most inspiring.

"Do you understand me now, Pierce? Your 'I AM' is about changing your thinking. It is about being the best and most successful version of yourself that you aspire to be—not imagining or fantasizing about it, but truly believing you embody it. Take another look at where and who you want to be and rework your 'I AM' statement over the weekend. Any time you catch yourself thinking differently from your statement, use the 'Reframe' exercise to reframe your thinking so that it aligns with your 'I AM' statement."

Dr. J. casually strolled to a small gray filing cabinet tucked in the corner of his office and withdrew three sheets of paper. Immediately recognizing them as more exercises to complete, Pierce protested, "I thought you said this was not about a bunch of exercises and techniques—I feel like that is all I am doing." Sounding like a whiney little boy who was told he could have no more birthday cake, Pierce stopped himself from saying anything further.

Placing the three sheets of paper on the table, Dr. J. calmly responded, "You're correct, Pierce, I did say that. What we are doing is utilizing some exercises and techniques as tools to direct you toward change. The techniques and exercises merely guide you to scratch the surface and/or help to keep you on track—the work has to happen deep within your psyche, deep within your core, and only you can do that."

"Understood." Pierce sat up a little straighter and leafed through the three pieces of paper.

YOUR "I AM" Statement

YOUR "I AM" Statements, are the answers to the "Who are YOU???" question. You have the ability to answer this question based on the person that you are or based on the person that you believe you have the talent to become.

Remember, the key is challenging yourself to think beyond the person that you currently are and the things that you have already achieved. Connect to the person you desire to be and grab your future and bring it to today.

I AM _____

I AM _____

I AM _____

I AM _____

I AM _____

I AM _____

YOUR Vision

YOUR Purpose statement _____

_____

_____

Personal goals _____

_____

_____

Professional goals _____

_____

_____

Reframe

When faced with adversity, REFRAME the negative response and choose the positive SOLUTION to keep YOU on YOUR path to greatness.

In the box below, identify a recent time in which you faced adversity or challenge and could have responded more favorably by focusing on solutions. Then, REFRAME your past reaction and identify the better response that would have kept you on a path to success.

Dr. J. watched as Pierce looked dejectedly at the first two pages. "I want you to refocus on YOUR 'I AM' statements—and YOUR Vision statement individually. I feel this may be a better initial approach for you."

Feeling tired and chastened, Pierce wanted nothing more than to go home and crawl back under the covers, but instead he asked about the third sheet of paper the doctor had placed in front of him. "So, how does this REFRAME technique work?"

"Ah, so glad you asked. I like to refer to it as recalibrating your thinking!" Dr. J. took his place on the sofa next to Pierce once again, "An artful yet complicated science!" He smiled directly at Pierce, who inched his way to the edge of the sofa, vying for a little space. "There is a psychology principle called *expectancy theory*. It speculates that what you focus on expands. If you focus on the negative, you attract more negative; if you *choose* to focus on the positive, you will attract more positive."

"Sure, I have heard of that." Pierce sat up a little straighter.

The doctor held a finger up and raised both eyebrows for dramatic effect. "When faced with an obstacle or adversity, simply make the choice to say '*REFRAME*,' and refocus your attention on a solution, within ninety seconds—rather than placing your focus on the negative, or choosing a reactive response to the problem itself."

"So if I am not thinking in line with my 'I AM' statements, or find myself caught up in old behaviors or thinking, I simply REFRAME?"

Dr. J. reached for Pierce's shoulder and gave it a congratulatory squeeze. "Yes, absolutely, this should be used as a tool to change the way you think. If you find yourself caught up in old thought patterns that do not serve you, simply say '*REFRAME*' and focus on thought patterns that are more aligned with your goals—and try to do so within ninety seconds, lest you get swept away ruminating on a train wreck."

"Okay."

"Brilliant!" Dr. J. gave Pierce's shoulder another squeeze. "You are getting this so quickly, Pierce. Just brilliant."

10

Effort and Results

Wins and losses come a dime a dozen.

But effort? Nobody can judge that.

Effort is between you and you.

—Ray Lewis

"Recalibrating your thoughts, what does that even mean?" Josh demanded as he and Pierce rounded the corner of the park, completing their third lap.

"I know; it sounds like quackery. But it actually works." Pierce wheezed, struggling to keep up with his extremely fit friend.

"Need me to slow down, buddy?"

"No! I'm fine," Pierce lied. "It's a question of being mindful of when you are slipping into old habits or thinking patterns; you catch yourself and redirect your thoughts to the new habits or more favorable thinking patterns."

"Kind of like doublethinking?" Josh was puzzled.

"More like thinking in two languages." Pierce rehearsed his brilliant analogy on Josh, the one he could not wait to share with Dr. J. the following morning. Having spent the weekend reframing his thoughts at every opportunity—of which there were many—Pierce came to understand that changing the way you think was not unlike learning a new language. While constantly thinking in your native language, you struggled to translate each word into that of the new language, and vice versa. Translating words to that of your native tongue in order to make sense of them was a lot of work. Though initially challenging, with study and time, you began to grasp the new language and might discover you began to *think* in the new language—thoughts occurred and were understood without the need for translation. Eventually, you began to dream in the new language; it was ingrained in you. You embodied it and all signs of struggle were gone.

"Boathouse? Burger and beer?" Josh's bushy eyebrows danced, quizzing Pierce. "Sound good?"

"Huh?" Startled from his reverie, Pierce had no idea what Josh had asked.

"Beer. Burger. Fuel?" Josh looked at his friend hopefully, indicating the little boathouse in the center of the park behind him. The thought of a burger and a beer after running four miles at Josh's pace made Pierce nauseated. But Sarah was at brunch with Belinda and the kids, and he did not want to dirty the kitchen making lunch for just one person. Besides, it had been a long time since he had spent real time with Josh.

"Beer and burger it is." Sweeping an arm toward the boathouse, he encouraged Josh to lead the way. Which Josh did, breaking out in a light jog that Pierce was grateful he could keep up with. Immediately summoning the waitress to bring some ice for his knee, Pierce could not wait to sit.

"Oh crap, your knee!" Josh slapped a sweaty palm across his own forehead. "You should have said something; we should have gone slower . . . walked, even. Oh man, I am so sorry I forgot."

"It's fine, it's fine . . . Really, it does me good to keep it moving."

"If you need to, ice it; it must be hurting."

"It is . . . a little, but it's all good, I want to keep it mobile—the run did me good anyway. Mentally I needed it; I've spent a lot of time inside my head this week and it was nice to get back into my body. Even if it is a little rusty."

"Work, huh? Back at the grind?"

"Actually, no—thank you." Pierce stopped to take the ice from the waitress, carefully arranging it on his knee. Josh ordered two burgers, medium-well with the works, and a couple of pints of Stella Artois for the two of them. "Water, too, please," Pierce called after her as she strolled off to punch the order into the MICROS system.

"What was I saying?—Oh yeah, work. No, I am taking a sabbatical from work."

Josh blinked rapidly. "Again? I ran into Sarah just last week, she said you were doing great, and were back at it—but with a fresh attitude and approach. Mission accomplished!"

"I was, until I realized that all I had learned on my journey merely provided the catalyst for change; the change itself was going to require a little more time and effort . . . more than I imagined, to be honest. I am on the path for sure, but far from mission accomplished."

Josh leaned back in his chair, examining his friend for a long moment. "Good for you," he finally said, his shaved head nodding in approval like a bald bobblehead toy.

"Water, please," Pierce used a firmer tone with the waitress as she placed two glistening pints of beer in front of the two friends. Josh gulped down half of his, replacing the sweating glass on the table with a satisfied sigh. Pierce nudged his further away and waited for water.

"Random question." Pierce asked, "Do you ever use goal-setting tools? You know, like a vision statement?"

Josh shrugged. "Sure, why?"

Pierce rearranged the ice pack, wiping a trickle of water that ran down his knee. Waving to the waitress, he mimed drinking out of an imaginary glass, reminding her, once again, to bring water. "I have an issue with it."

"Who, the waitress?"

"Nooo—well, yes, if she doesn't bring me my damn water soon, I will! And so will her tip! But . . . the vision statement stuff, it seems kind of hokey to me. THANK *YOU*," Pierce said to the waitress who had finally brought him his water. He resented the sarcasm in his voice; the poor kid could be no more than sixteen and was probably lost in thought about a wayward boyfriend or something. But, seriously, he needed water and had almost finished the entire glass before she timidly slunk away. Her shy awkwardness reminded him of his daughter and served to tame his sarcasm. *She's just a kid*, he thought, stopping himself from making a scene and demanding more water. Savoring the last third of his glass with careful sips, he would wait until she served his burger to ask for more.

"My company uses vision statements all of the time," Josh said.

"They do?!" Pierce was surprised. Josh ran a large account division at Northwestern Mutual, and it made sense that a company of its caliber would introduce goal-setting exercises to its employees—especially personnel who were managing and acquiring accounts. But it still felt oddly hokey to him, and he imagined a conservative entity such as Northwestern would not dare venture into hokeyness.

"Of course we do. Vision statements, goal setting—whatever you want to call it, it is *not* 'hokey' and certainly not new age—there are studies from *Harvard* in the *seventies* warranting the practice. Companies like ours—in fact, all of the big hitters—utilize these techniques on a regular basis. Where have you been, hiding out in a cave somewhere?" He playfully nudged Pierce's shoulder.

"Apparently, yes," Pierce conceded, eyeing the two juicy burgers arriving at their table. Gently placing a hand on the waitress's forearm to get her attention, he said, "Be a doll and bring two more large glasses of water, would you?"

"And another beer." Josh raised his empty pint glass in the general direction of the waitress before turning to Pierce. "Did you just call her doll? You really *have* been living in a cave, haven't you?"

The waitress returned with two glasses of water and a fresh pint of lager for Josh. "Could I borrow a pen?" Josh asked the young girl, who silently plunged her hand deep in the front pocket of her apron to retrieve a pen for him.

After taking a bite of his burger, Josh smoothed out a napkin, wrote two words in its center, and drew a neat circle around them. Exchanging the pen for his burger, he took another healthy bite.

Squinting and turning his head ninety degrees to read what Josh had written, he saw that it looked like a name. "Andre Welder?" Pierce asked.

Nodding, Josh washed down his third bite with a gulp of beer, wiped his mouth with the back of his hand and reached for the pen. "Hall of Famer—Northwestern brings him in once or twice a year to talk to our group about the value of goal setting."

"Seriously?" Pierce felt ready to listen. Of all the work Dr. J. had given him over the week, this exercise had eluded him almost as much as the 'I AM' statement. Now his best friend was warranting a similar method—in fact, it appeared, was singing its praises—as did the legendary Andre Welder.

"Circa 1986, as a junior at Northern State, fueled by a burning desire to play football, Andre walked on to the team. Attending a small rural high school often overlooked by scouts, Andre was held back by a crippling fear of rejection during his first two years of college. Athletically, nobody knew who the kid was. By his junior year, Andre could no longer fight the overwhelming desire to play football that burned in the pit of his gut, so he took a ballsy chance and walked on to the team. It goes without saying he got the coaches' attention. During his senior year, a year after walking on and succeeding as a valuable asset to Northern State, Andre pondered his future. Knowing he wanted to play in the NFL, he began to map out his future." Unfolding the napkin, Josh wrote furiously before passing the paper across the table to Pierce.

1. I will play for an NFL team and lead my team to the Super Bowl.

2. I will play in such a way that my coaches will benefit (e.g., promotions, higher salaries, etc.).

3. I will be recognized as one of the greatest cornerbacks to play in the NFL.

Pierce had an eerie sense of déjà vu. Looking across the table at his lifelong buddy, he made the connection—Josh channeled equal parts of Coach E. *and* Dr. J., and it kind of freaked Pierce out. Reading the list of goals scrawled on the napkin in front of him, Pierce was transported to the little sports bar in St. Louis where he first met Coach E. The goals listed on the piece of paper in his hands echoed elements of Coach E.'s technique, *YOUR Prizefighter Day*. And it had nothing to do with them being scrawled on a napkin. They were completely different exercises, but Pierce noted parallels between Andre Welder's college-age life-goal list and Coach E.'s philosophy on setting three daily activity goals:

1. Personal—I will be recognized as one of the greatest players to play in the NFL HALL of FAME.

2. Business—I will lead my team to the Super Bowl.

3. Service—I will play in such a way that my coaches will benefit (e.g., promotions, higher salaries, etc.).

"You need me to tell you what happened next?" Josh's voice cut through Pierce's thoughts, snapping him back to the moment.

"I have a feeling you are going to anyway." Pierce finally reached for his beer, leaned back, and took a long, cool sip.

"Andre Welder, as you know, is without a doubt one of the most celebrated cornerbacks in the history of the NFL." Josh tapped his knuckles on the napkin he had scribbled all over. "He systematically achieved each goal on his list—a list he wrote in his *senior* year of college. He wrote down three goals, did not distract himself with doubt or fear, but instead pursued those goals with an equal and unwavering belief in himself and his ability to achieve them. Drafted into the NFL immediately upon graduation, he enjoyed a fourteen-year career, playing in eight Pro Bowls and, eventually, the 2001 Super Bowl."

"And now he travels the world pumping up the Northwestern Mutual sales divisions in each corner of the globe?"

Josh responded by tossing a balled up napkin at his friend. "Mockery will get you nowhere, grasshopper."

Catching the napkin in his left hand, Pierce set it to the side of the table. "Here is my problem with this exercise. Well, one of them . . . first of all, I struggle with the one-year and five-year thing."

Josh's eyebrows knitted together, a bushy arrow pointing to the top of his shiny head.

"I don't get the point of those two time markers specifically—what about the second and third and fourth year—why leap from one to five? And then, what about the mechanics of the first year—shouldn't there be a month by month plan to get there?"

Josh's face broke into a huge smile. "Dude, you're overthinking it! The 'mechanics,' the 'how,' is irrelevant. It's what you want to achieve and the BELIEF that you can achieve it that matters."

"And the timing?"

"There is no golden rule to the chronological spacing of your goals; that's completely subjective, so long as it resonates with and makes sense to you. Look at Andre's—he did not even put a timeline on his!" Waving the napkin under Pierce's nose, Josh drove his point home.

Pensive, Pierce once again realized he had been too regimented, too literal in his thinking. Was this the reason Dr. J.'s exercise had caused him so much inner turmoil? By failing to understand that he could space goals in any chronology that suited him, did he simply get stuck trying to come up with a one-year and five-year vision that did not resonate with him? He knew that was part of it, and Josh's explanation certainly made him feel a little better about at least giving the task another shot.

"What's really bugging me is that YOU know about this—and practice it, right?"

"Yes."

"All of these mentors I keep stumbling upon—the coach in St. Louis I told you about, the new shrink I am seeing . . . er, working with." Saying it out loud, Pierce was suddenly self-conscious that *he* was seeing a psychologist. Swallowing the bitter bile of foolish pride, he continued, "If these techniques are as valuable as they are purported to be, two things perplex me. One: How, by the age of 42, did these theories pass me by? And, Two: How—not to brag—did I find so much success in life without utilizing them?" Feeling smug, Pierce leaned back in his chair with his beer and waited for Josh's answer.

"It's not rocket science, nor will you find these methods listed on the MBA curriculum, I agree. But, Pierce, I am your best friend and I love you, buddy, so please forgive me when I tell you this . . . You probably *have* been introduced to these techniques by somebody before and dismissed them or chosen not to listen." Quite accustomed to people pointing out what an ass he had been, Pierce found Josh's comment mildly amusing. Josh was surprised to see a bemused smirk spread across his friend's face, rather than the expected burst of indignation.

"Go on." Pierce's smirk turned into a full-blown smile of encouragement. Josh took the final bite of his burger, balled the napkin up, and tossed it onto the empty plate in front of him. Waving to the waitress across the room, he pointed to his empty pint glass and made a "V" sign with his fingers, indicating she should bring two more. Pierce did not protest. On the cusp of experiencing yet another moment of truth, the anesthetic qualities of the alcohol would likely help to calm and soothe the sting of facing "old Pierce."

"Buddy, you *are* successful. Always have been, you work damn hard and deserve it. But, think about it . . . When you are successful, it is very easy to fall into the trap of not examining yourself. Why would you? You're successful, right?"

Pierce shrugged, "If it ain't broken, why fix it?"

"Exactly," Josh enthused. "Exactly where the pitfall lies! You are succeeding at work, yet failing at life!" Ouch! Pierce looked around for the waitress and her pint of pain repellent.

"Come on, this is no surprise to you. Your journey, working with—what's his name—Dr. J.? Why would you be searching for these answers now if you truly believed that you were succeeding in all facets of life?" Pierce nodded conceding the truth. As harsh as it sounded, Josh summed it up perfectly; Pierce had been succeeding at work, yet failing at life. And Josh, like most of those close to Pierce, was unaware he had also come alarmingly close to failing at work, single-handedly causing the failure of his company's merger. The importance of completing each step in this work resonated with Pierce, and he felt ready to head home and tackle his goal-setting exercise.

11

Leaps and Bounds: Sessions with Dr. J.

If you want to feel better about the direction you are headed, bear down and go to work.

—Dr. Jason Selk

Session #3
Monday, November 17, 2014
8:00 a.m.

The bright morning sun shone through the bay windows, blinding Pierce. It was amazing how during the fall season, in just three days' time, the position of the sun could change so dramatically—chasing warm winds and lifting birds on their southern pilgrimage. Dr. J. puttered about in the kitchenette, brewing his customary pot of green tea, as Pierce tried his new language analogy out on his mentor.

"Yes, indeed!" Dr. J. enthused.

"Well, the more I worked on myself this weekend, the more I came to realize it is considerably more complex than that—akin to experiencing and embracing an entirely new and foreign culture."

"Ah," said Dr. J., lowering himself right beside Pierce on the tiny European sofa once again. "You are beginning to grasp the depth of the process; your analogy is spot-on. Anybody can listen to some tapes and learn a language, but to understand the culture, to really grasp it, one must be immersed in it."

"Oh, I'm immersed."

"Indeed you are. So, tell me about your weekend. Clearly you experienced a breakthrough in your comprehension . . . but I have never doubted your ability to *understand*. How about the work itself? Were there any *obstacles*?"

Pierce shrugged. Dr. J. had a point. Once again, without realizing it, Pierce had spent a lot of time and energy intellectualizing—sure, he had also done the work, yet it was evident his eagerness to prove he understood the theory outweighed his desire to delve into the questions that arose from his reflection. Or, to put it bluntly, to admit there were things he did not know or understand.

"I guess that's a breakthrough," Pierce said, smiling.

"Hmmm." Dr. J. cocked his head to one side, waiting for Pierce to go on.

"Seems my priority this morning was to prove what I know rather than explore what I do not."

"Very well, so let's play a little game." Not one for games, Pierce preferred to get to the point. Knowing he had no alternative, he reluctantly surrendered to Dr. J. "I want you to walk out of my office, down the hall to the elevator bank. Once there, count to ten very slowly before strolling back and entering my room as if for the first time this morning. Call it a "reframe" for the day. We'll start fresh and see if we can't nip that old habit of yours in the bud."

Pierce loathed Dr. J. for making him play act. Self-consciously skulking along the hall like a fool, he frantically patted his pockets with both hands when he arrived at the elevator bank, pretending to have forgotten something on the off chance a random stranger had witnessed his bizarre, destination-less act of walking up and down the hall.

Reentering Dr. J.'s office, no longer hiding behind a mask of intellect, felt highly unnatural and awkward, yet oddly *refreshing*. Quirky Dr. J. was stripping away Pierce's armor and getting straight to the heart of his truth. As foolish as he felt, Pierce knew he was making leaps and bounds, pushing beyond understanding to simply "being," or, as he had put it earlier, not just speaking the lingo but embodying the culture.

"Good morning, Pierce!" Dr. J. leapt from the sofa, genuinely happy to see Pierce and truly behaving as if it was for the first time that day. *Is he really taking it this far?* Pierce thought to himself, reaching his right hand out to shake Dr. J.'s.

"Good morning, Dr. J., great to see you." *Yes*, he thought, *we both are*.

The two men spent the better part of the session reviewing Pierce's I AM Statements and Vision Statements. Dr. J. agreed with and applauded Pierce's realization that he had gotten caught in the inflexible thinking trap, affirming Josh's point that the chronology of the extended one- or five-year Vision Statement was less important than the belief in one's ability to attain the goals set forth.

Pierce then produced a copy of Coach E.'s *Prizefighter Day*. "So, which is better; which should I focus on?" Pierce asked Dr. J.

"I'm sorry?"

"YOUR *Prizefighter Day* or Vision Statements—which should I practice? Which is better?"

"Ah, inflexible thinking rears its ugly head once again."

At a loss for words, Pierce waited for Dr. J. to fill the silence. "Both are valuable, Pierce. One sets forth where you want to be and helps you to believe with all your heart that you are already there. BUT, with day-to-day distractions, it is possible to lose sight of that belief. The second exercise—the one your beloved Coach E. showed you—pertains to *daily* activity-goal-setting practice to keep you connected to your maximum effort *and* on the right path, not only to your vision but to being the best person you can be each and every day."

"So I need to stick with both?"

Pointing to the vision statement Pierce had completed the evening prior, Dr. J. asked, "Pierce, are you committed to what you wrote there?"

"Of course."

"Life is going to happen, and there are days it will take you way off course. Exercises like the one Coach E. gave you serve to keep you on track."

"But isn't that then being focused on or clutching at results?"

"Not at all. Listen, you will have days, despite your best intentions, when the results you crave elude you. Yet you will feel successful because you did everything in your power to work toward your goal. Daily activity focus—*daily work*—is imperative to staying on course. It keeps you accountable and on track—it is the driving force behind your ultimate success."

Pierce looked at his watch. He was tired of thinking; the only thing he craved was to be out on College Street in the sunshine and fresh air.

"Let's wrap it up with a final thought for the day. You told me a story about Andre Welder earlier. He eventually achieved all three goals he had set for himself in his senior year of college, correct?"

Pierce nodded.

"Not merely a sports psychologist, I happen to be a sports fanatic. In 2001, Andre Welder's team lost 32–29. But as you told the story to me, Andre continues to recognize and list this as a victory. And he should! Achieving what he set out to do, he led his team to the Super Bowl. They did not get the desired result, yet Andre Welder does not view it as failure. Would you?"

"But did he focus on it every day?" Pierce's defiance inflated, a giant balloon of resistance.

"On belief, yes. On the results, absolutely not." A warm, sharp pin swiftly deflated doubt, replacing it with pure clarity.

Stepping out onto College Street, Pierce felt an immense sense of freedom stir within. The sun's warmth was a sharp contrast to the crisp fall air that whipped around him; Pierce broke into a gentle jog to counter it. Incredibly light and no longer burdened by his armor or questions, Pierce broke into a run. For the first time in weeks, his knee did not bother him. He felt amazing.

12

Exploring Legacy: Sessions with Dr. J.

We don't inherit the earth from our ancestors, we borrow it from our children.

—David Brower

Session #4

Tuesday, November 18, 2014
8:00 a.m.

"Do you like college basketball?"

"S-sure." Pierce was surprised by the random question.

"Fabulous! Do you have plans this Friday evening?"

"N-noo, not that I can recall." Not wanting to walk into the trap of committing to something he really did not want to do, Pierce trod with extreme care.

"Perfect. Duke University is hosting a charity basketball event this week. Furman is playing Friday night, against St. Louis University, I believe. Anderson and Molly Phillips invited me to join them, but I have a conflict—my niece is getting married Friday evening." Dr. J. shrugged, one of those 'Ech—what can ya do?' kind of shrugs. "Would you like to attend the game in my place?"

Pierce nodded, "I should check with my wife, but I am sure it will be fine. And thank you for thinking of me." Pierce had never socialized with Anderson outside of work. Since Anderson was his new commander-in-chief, it was about time Pierce got to know him personally. Meditating on the importance of forging a bond with Anderson, he began to wonder if Dr. J.'s niece really was getting married . . . Friday night weddings were rather uncommon, if not unique. Orchestrated or not, Pierce recognized it was an extremely good idea and accepted the invitation gracefully, surrendering the ruse of checking with Sarah, who he knew would encourage the outing.

"So, what are we working on today?" Dr. J. asked.

"The final piece of the puzzle. Legacy."

"Legacy. Why is legacy a puzzle to you, Pierce?"

"Well, there appears to be too much focus on it. To me, legacy is a result and something you leave behind when you die. Can you really focus on something like that? How can you control what people will think of you when you die? Adding to the confusion, my fourth mentor, Dr. Barnes, touted the creation of a Living Legacy. She insisted I focus on it every day."

"I see." Dr. J. stared off for a moment, processing Pierce's words. After a long beat he turned to Pierce, "The Living Legacy statement you provided me last week, this was what your fourth mentor gave you, yes?"

"Uh-huh."

"You read hers and felt inspired, but when it came to writing your own you couldn't wrap your head around it, am I correct?" Pierce sat up straight. Dr. J. was dead right; he nailed it. As Pierce was leaving Boston several weeks ago, he believed he had grasped what Dr. Barnes meant by her philosophy of creating a Living Legacy—despite initially struggling with it during their conversation. Explaining her interpretation and showing him her own Living Legacy statement, Dr. Barnes made it seem easy. But when Pierce attempted to work through it on his own, he merely filled it by noting his top five philosophies in life. Somehow it did not resonate with him as *LEGACY*; merely a list of other peoples' philosophies and nothing of his own.

"Legacy is such a BIG word. One of those big, old, heavy-hitter words that carries a lot of weight—along with equal parts mysticism and misinterpretation. Not unlike the word 'guru.'" Pierce looked to Dr. J., hoping he was making sense.

"Which part did you get stuck on, Pierce? The weight, the mysticism, or the misinterpretation?"

Pierce leaned forward and spoke in a low whisper, "The idea of legacy seems so big to me. Too big, and I am afraid I don't live up to it."

"Let me ask you something, Pierce, and don't answer right away; soak up my question and think about it." Pierce nodded. "If you died today, do you feel you have achieved enough in your life—by this I mean worked hard with honor and integrity, served others, community involvement, etc.—to leave an impression that would inspire others to do the same?"

Only last week, Pierce's idea of serving others had been cutting Sarah loose from the responsibility of taking the kids to school. There was no denying he was a hard worker . . . yet he failed to balance work, play, and family—the very trigger for this self-exploration journey. Community? Pierce collapsed back in the sofa in defeat. He had a long way to go.

"Rose Barnes's exercises are a good start to begin defining what you would like your legacy to be, Pierce. An excellent start, in fact. I looked at your responses—the philosophies and people you have learned from and been impacted by the most, those that have driven you to enjoy the success you have achieved so far. This all counts as legacy—*wisdom* you can pass on the next generation."

"I just feel *legacy* should be something bigger than that."

"Than what?"

"Wisdom." Pierce's voice felt small, like a six-year-old boy's.

"It can be bigger than that. It can be whatever you want it to be." Dr. J. smiled kindly at Pierce. "You used the analogy of a guru to highlight the mysticism and room for interpretation surrounding legacy. Did you know that the word *guru* simply means *teacher*?

"You are your own guru, your own teacher," Dr. J. continued. "You create YOUR own legacy. All of the exercises we have approached over this past week are merely an endeavor to uncover your truth. The path you ultimately choose to take, and the destination it leads to, depends on how much work you want to do, how much you believe in yourself, and how focused you remain. Define what you would like your legacy to be, believe you can achieve it, and work—every day—toward building your legacy. Exactly. How. You. Want. It. To. Be."

Leaving Dr. J.'s office, Pierce only felt slightly more certain of what legacy meant to him. Compared with the clarity and sense of elation he achieved in yesterday's session, today he left feeling disappointed and heavy.

13

Understanding YOUR Legacy

It's not how long you live. It's how you

choose to live your life.

—Janet Fishman Newman

Duke University

Friday, November 21, 2014

Anderson was barely recognizable, wearing neat, dark blue jeans and his purple Furman jersey. Pierce had never seen him out of business attire; he looked about ten years younger. His wife, Molly, looked younger and prettier than Pierce recalled, too. Making their way through the stands of Cameron Indoor Stadium and to their seats, Pierce was overwhelmed by the turnout. It had been years since he attended a college game, and the enthusiasm of the youth filing into the stadium was electric.

"Beer? Pretzels? Popcorn? Soda?" A young man with a long braid trailing down his back called out, carefully climbing the steps alongside their seats, his brown eyes barely visible over the edge of the plastic tub holding beers, soda, and ice. Clipped bags of popcorn and pretzels dangled precariously from two poles attached to the plastic tub. Pierce recalled, with a tinge of guilt, how easily he breezed through college without the need of a laborious part-time job to supplement his income.

"Want anything?" Anderson asked, indicating the young man and his wares.

"Please, allow me." Pierce fished in his pocket for his wallet with one hand and waved the hawker down with his free one. "Molly, what would you like?"

Molly shrugged. "I'll take a Bud Light. Thanks, Pierce!"

"Anderson?"

"Same. Thanks, buddy."

"Three Bud Lights, please." The young man gladly placed his heavy plastic tub on the ground beside them, shrugged his stiff shoulders a few times, and passed three plastic bottles of beer to Pierce.

"Thirty dollars." Braid boy smiled.

"*Thir*—Okay." Thumbing through his wallet, Pierce found three ten-dollar bills and three additional singles. Feeling guilty and embarrassed that a ten percent tip may appear cheap to his hosts, he added two extra singles.

"Thanks." Braid boy lifted his tub with a hop and skip and disappeared into the sea of purple jerseys once again, "Beer? Pretzels? Popcorn? Soda?"

Replacing the wallet in his back pocket Pierce passed the beers along to his new friends.

"Daylight robbery, huh?" Anderson laughed, taking the sweating bottles from Pierce.

"Worse than Disneyland!" Pierce exclaimed.

"So glad you could join us, Pierce." Molly held her bottle up to make a toast.

"Me too, thank you, both of you." He smiled, tapping the neck of his bottle to theirs, and made a mental note to get some more cash from the ATM in case they wanted another round. Taking in the painted faces, costumes, and wigs around the stadium, Pierce thought it was more akin to a Halloween party than a charity basketball match—he almost felt out of place in his neat khaki pants and new Furman T-shirt Sarah had thoughtfully picked up the previous day.

"Pope having any luck securing new contracts in Europe market?" Although he hadn't intended to bring up work, Pierce was at a loss for a conversation starter—he had never talked about anything else with Anderson.

"Uh-uh boys, NO shop talk." Molly smiled cheerily, raising her eyebrows at her husband when she thought Pierce was not looking. Pretending not to notice her look while desperately searching for something to say, Pierce was saved when the stadium broke into applause, shattering what was shaping up to be an awkward moment.

As he looked around trying to find what the fuss was about, Pierce's eyes finally settled on the highly polished, hard maple court. One after another, teenage boys in wheelchairs wheeled themselves onto the court. The crowd jumped to their feet in a heartfelt standing ovation, getting louder and louder, as the teens wheeled themselves into position, lining up in a prime courtside position between the SLU and Furman coaching tables.

"Who are those kids?" Pierce asked Anderson and Molly, not once taking his eyes off the teens, nor the rambunctious crowd's outpouring of love and respect for these young men.

"Atlanta Hawks—junior wheelchair basketball team. They played a charity game here last night, wiping the floor with their opponents. As you can see, they were a huge hit with the home crowd."

Lamely, Pierce thought about his knee and how disadvantaged he felt using Jon's cane. Looking at these young men, smiling and waving to the crowd, riding the high of a huge win at a sport they clearly loved, it was apparent they did not see themselves as disadvantaged at all; they embraced who they were and overcame life's adversities with positivity and passion. Being wheelchair-bound did not stop them from finding their passion—basketball. And it certainly did not stop them from excelling at it. Each of them had earned a position on a league team, traveling the country and playing—it seemed—to an incredibly receptive crowd.

"Inspirational." Pierce surprised himself when his thought leaked out of his mouth.

"You bet! They played an unbelievable game," Anderson responded.

Molly leaned in adding, "Our son, Paul, got us in to meet with the team before the game, and they were so fired up. Honestly, they were no different from Furman prior to a game. The chairs were the only difference in the locker room, and after spending less than a minute with these young men, you no longer see the chairs, only dedicated boys playing a sport they love, in true team spirit."

"I had no idea . . ." Pierce trailed off, not knowing what to say. He had no idea about a lot of things lately—why be surprised that he had no idea there was a national wheelchair basketball league? Why be surprised that there were human beings out there, so much younger, yet so much more evolved than he? Why be surprised by anything?

Leaping to their feet once again, the crowd went crazy as the SLU and Furman team members and coaches were announced.

Each player, from each team, first ran along the side of the court high-fiving the Atlanta Hawks before taking their position on the court. No contrived act of compassion and most definitely not pity, it was a genuine act of admiration and awe. Pierce was beginning to regret the fact he was not aware of and had missed the previous evening's game. It must have been thrilling.

"That's our Paul!" Molly beamed with pride, pointing a slender finger toward a tall gangly kid sporting a dirty-dishwater blonde crew cut. Pierce could see that placing Paul and Anderson side by side would be like one of those photo-aging software gimmicks; they were identical, save the thirtyish-year age difference.

"I can see that!" Pierce smiled broadly at Molly. Beginning to relax, he really was glad that he decided to come—for many reasons.

* * *

Furman did not share the Atlanta Hawks' luck on the court that evening, losing by six points to SLU. "Eh, it was a charity game," Anderson said with a shrug.

"Great game! Furman held their own, just got unlucky at the end there," Pierce offered.

"Ya know SLU has a strong team this year; I think they're gonna do really well." Anderson pointed down to the court toward the team from St. Louis. "You hear about their legendary coach, Majerus?"

"Of course!" Everybody knew Rick Majerus! A colorful college basketball coach who enjoyed a career coaching at Marquette—where he initially tried out for the team himself as a walk-on in 1967—as well as Ball State, University of Utah, and finally Saint Louis University, Majerus was highly respected and regarded as one of the sharpest minds in sports history. Pierce also knew that the beloved coach had passed away several years earlier at the age of sixty-four, from heart failure.

"Not long before he passed away, Majerus boldly stated to a journalist that the Billikens would be a top-ten team within three years. Insisting he had achieved similar success with Ball State and Utah, he intended to coach the Billikens to a top-ten position. And you know what? He did." Anderson stared at the SLU team, who had just beaten his own son's team, with a look of pride etched on his face.

"Just twenty-three months after making that statement, less than two years after he died, *and* on what would have been Majerus's sixty-sixth birthday, SLU moved to a coveted top ten position for the first time since the 1964–65 season."

"Wow." Once again, Pierce was speechless. One coach's unwavering belief in his team impacted their success beyond the grave. *Dare to believe*, Pierce thought to himself. *It clearly does make a difference.*

Anderson placed a hand on Pierce's shoulder, ushering him toward the main aisle. "They're definitely a team to keep your eye on this season. Them and Furman, of course!"

"Pierce, would you like to come down to the locker room and meet Paul?" Molly asked as they reached the main entrance to the stadium.

"Sure, that would be great!" A flutter of excitement at the prospect of meeting the Furman team arose, taking Pierce by surprise. Secretly harboring the hope that the Atlanta Hawks wheelchair team would be down there too, he eagerly trailed Molly and Anderson through the crowds of purple and white faces, smudged with beer, sweat, and melancholy.

Momentarily somber in mood, the Furman team sat in

a huddle with their coaches, discussing the game. Once the meeting broke, the somber mood disappeared to be replaced by the resilience of youth and enthusiasm as players cheerfully greeted parents, friends, and guests.

Confident and mature beyond his years, Paul seemed genuinely interested in meeting his father's boss and the man behind BlackBird Tech. Pierce was reminded that most young men, not unlike himself, never let go of that boyhood fascination with planes or the aero industry.

"Do you have kids in school too?" Paul asked.

"Sure, a little younger than you though. I have two. Lila is six and Max is four."

"Oh, wow! Does your boy like basketball?"

"I guess." Pierce shrugged. Max had not yet settled on any particular sport. "He's a little young, but doesn't every kid love basketball?"

Anderson's doppelganger nodded his head enthusiastically. "Yes sir! Hey, how about I get the team to sign a ball for your boy?"

"Wow, that would be great. Thanks!"

"How about I go one better and get the SLU team to sign it too? The captain of the team is a good buddy of mine." Paul smiled Anderson's broad, wide-toothed grin. If not for such an open and disarming smile, the likeness would have been eerily creepy.

"That . . . that would be great; thank you, Paul." Pierce was touched by Paul's eagerness to provide inspiration to his own little boy. "If you could get the Atlanta team to sign too, we'll have a trifecta."

Paul cocked his head to one side and raised an eyebrow. "You saw them play? Weren't they awesome?"

Pierce raised his palm and shook his head regretfully. "Unfortunately, no. I did not make it last night. Sounds like I missed some game, huh?"

"Oh, yeah! They were on *fire*! You know, we are heading over to McDuff's for a post-event party tonight. You should come. The Atlanta team will be there as well."

"Wow! If that's okay, I would love to!" Pierce hoped Molly and Anderson would not mind him tagging along.

"No problemo; let me go get that ball." Paul winked and smiled, walking off toward the locker room exit.

"Leave space for the Atlanta team's signatures!" Pierce called after him, to which Paul replied by thrusting an extra-large thumb toward the ceiling. Dr. J. had been correct in his assessment of Paul, who truly was an exceptional young man.

14

Inspiring Legacy and Greatness in Others

I believe our legacy will be defined by the accomplishments and fearless nature by which our daughters and sons take on the global challenges we face. I also wonder if perhaps the most lasting expression of one's humility lies in our ability to foster and mentor our children.

—Naveen Jain

Arriving home a little after midnight, Pierce quietly made his way upstairs to the bedroom. Stealthily stealing his way past Max's open door, he squeezed the basketball tucked under his arm a little closer; he could not wait to give it to Max the following morning!

Slipping under the covers next to Sarah, she softly murmured, "How was the game?"

"Amazing." He kissed the back of her head. "Really amazing."

"Didn't they lose?" Puzzled, Sarah had obviously watched the televised event, playing spot-Daddy-in-the-crowd with Lila and Max.

"Yes and no." Pierce answered truthfully—both he and the entire Furman team had been in the presence of true greatness (the Atlanta Hawks wheelchair team) and legacy (Majerus and his winning SLU team) tonight, and for this experience he considered them all winners.

"You're crazy." Sarah sighed, falling back into the soft embrace of slumber.

"Good night," Pierce whispered to the cool night air. *A very, very good night indeed*, he thought as he lay there smiling at the ceiling.

* * *

Epiphanies, *true epiphanies*, are rare and precious jewels. Pierce had experienced his fair share of them lately, but the epiphany he experienced as he passed Max his new basketball was the crowning jewel. The internal work he had strived to complete with Dr. J., his struggle with grasping what legacy actually meant to him, all culminated in a poignant moment of clarity and understanding. Covered in the scrawled and scribbly mess only a black Sharpie and the signatures of *three* great basketball teams could make, the ball was barely recognizable as a basketball. Yet, in this moment, Pierce realized he was giving his son so much more than a ball. It *was* LEGACY. Unquestionably, Pierce had struggled greatly with something that was extremely simple and right under his nose: he had been creating legacy as he was working on making positive changes within himself. His legacy was alive not only in the lessons learned but the core values he would pass on to his son and daughter. Inspiring them to be the best people they can be, despite the odds, despite any obstacles that may come their way.

Once again, Pierce had been thinking too big. He squeezed his tiny son tighter, appreciative of just how big the small things actually are. Looking over Max's shoulder, he caught a glimpse of Lila watching on, a forlorn expression on her pale freckled face. Releasing Max from his embrace he reached for her.

"I have a gift for you too Lila." Sarah eyed him carefully, giving him a worried look that screamed *you better*, lest he disappoint their fragile daughter yet again. "The Atlanta Hawks wheelchair team I was telling you about needs sponsorship—help with some money—to enable their team to continue playing at national tournaments. Last night I agreed to sponsor them, not as BlackBird Tech but as a private donor in your names!"

Lila looked unimpressed. Sometimes Pierce forgot she was just six years old. "Wait here," he ordered, before running back upstairs.

Returning quickly, Pierce approached Lila with his hands behind his back. Her eyes glowed with hope. "Yours and Max's names will appear on a special board at the team headquarters in Atlanta *and* in each and every program given to audiences who come to watch the team play . . . *AND* the four of us can go to any game the Atlanta Hawks play, anywhere in the country, with full access to the team and their cool mascot Harry the Hawk!" With that Pierce pulled a stuffed animal from behind his back—a medium-size plush toy of Harry the Hawk, thankfully given to him by the team's coach at the party last night. While it was not the most attractive stuffed animal when compared with the explosion of pink fluff in Lila's bedroom, Lila squealed with delight, hugging the bird as if it were all she had ever wanted. And in a way, this kind of attention from her father *was* all that she ever wanted.

Stepping back, taking in his happy family, picking at pancakes around the kitchen island on an overcast early winter Saturday, Pierce knew that Lila and Max would not understand the gravity of his gift until much later in life. Not grandiose, nor flashy, his gift might not stand out immediately in their memories as they grow into young adults, but oh, what a precious gift it was. Having Lila and Max sponsor this team was placing them at the forefront of greatness, providing a source of inspiration and a strong sense of community in his children from a young and impressionable age. And if Pierce continued to work as hard on himself as he intended, he hoped to continue to evolve, providing a constant source of inspiration for his children along the way.

* * *

Later that morning a FedEx truck arrived at Pierce's home, delivering a medium-size package addressed to Pierce. Assuming it was paperwork from the Atlanta Hawks to finalize his sponsorship, he was surprised to note the return address listed Dr. J.'s office. Tearing the package open he found a nest, a handwritten note, and a signed Wilson football.

Pierce,

YOU are an inspiration. Release YOUR greatness!
Max Effort Pays Off,

Dr. J.

P.S. Thank YOU for inspiring me—I updated the YOUR Legacy Statement I give clients to include some of your exercises! Take a look and let me know what you think.

Peering into the box, he retrieved the *YOUR Legacy State-ment* and was touched to see it now included inspiration from Coach E.'s *Prizefighter Day*. "Inspiring greatness in others" was the coach's motto, and he certainly had achieved that. Noticing the unmistakable scrawl of an autograph, Pierce excitedly removed the ball from the box. It was signed by Wes Camden, the now NFL star who believed wholeheartedly in his performance abilities and persevered through pain to get the attention of scouts at his pro day. As Pierce held the ball in his hands, he was reminded that he also had a daily choice to persevere and keep fighting the good fight.

Reading the inscription Wes had made before his signature, Pierce smiled knowingly. "LEAVE YOUR LEGACY." Now he and his son both had special inspiration to build their futures and legacies for many generations to come.

Exercises for YOUR Path to Greatness

Five Key Factors for Attaining Belief in Yourself

1. **Accept the truth:** Realizing and identifying with the person you are today is the key to becoming the person you want to be. Remember the lesson Pierce learned: we never actually *fail* in life. We just don't always get the results that we want. You cannot live a lie. You have to acknowledge and identify with what is most important in your life to ultimately attain belief in yourself.

2. **Speak the truth:** You may be reluctant—even scared—to talk about or acknowledge past behavior and habits that you regret. However, avoiding it only serves to amplify the pain and make us feel like victims. Get the truth out into the light by talking about your experiences with a trusted friend or a professional.

3. **Breathe through the truth:** Even though every fiber of your being wants to react by believing that your actions up to this point have been correct, know that you can change. Avoid acting from a place of pain or anger. The best way to reclaim your dignity is to behave rationally and treat yourself lovingly—which will keep you from self-destructing.

4. **Process the truth:** Give yourself time and space to find your equilibrium. Believe confidently and wholeheartedly that making these changes will prompt you to develop a stronger foundation. However, recognize that this will take time—and give yourself that time.

5. **Create a plan based on the truth:** Don't expect things to be perfect right away; you can't simply flip a switch and have a new life. Old behaviors and mindsets often come back into the realm. Stay strong and acknowledge that you must continue to believe and actively engage in this process in order to experience concrete change for your future. With this in mind, define how you want to live your life from now on.

Take out a piece of paper and write down any idea about the person you want to be and the life you want to live. Once you have clarity on this, you can take concrete steps toward realizing your goals and *attaining belief in yourself.*

YOUR
PRIZEFIGHTER DAY

Choosing Passion for the Process over Results: Create YOUR Prizefighter Day!

The world we live in today has become so complex—it moves so fast. Financial markets are up and down. We have pressures from work. We face obstacles with friends and family and the natural ebb and flow of life. What if there was a way that you could target EACH and EVERY day as a victory by focusing on daily activities rather than trying to hold on too tightly to results that you can't control?

Several years ago, I realized that when I felt stressed and anxious, it was usually a culmination of intense focus on the *results* of the tasks at hand rather than focusing on being passionate about the *process* of what I was doing. I developed a process called *YOUR Prizefighter Day* to give individuals the opportunity to make every single day a triumph. Here comes *YOUR Prizefighter Day*. Every single day can be a victory if that's what you choose. The most successful individuals find great success when they focus on having a passion for the process and they drive their daily behaviors.

The key: Identify three things that are activity driven for you and your life that if you accomplish today, will make today victorious (regardless of any obstacles that come your way). According to individuals from around the country who have successfully implemented these ongoing goals, they choose one that's personal, one that's business- or athletic-related, and one that's all about helping someone else.

1. **Personal activity example**: waking up every morning and getting in your morning workout because it makes you feel good (endorphins) and confident (strong) about your ability to go out and do great things.

2. **Business-related example** (in a sales career): setting a specific goal for the number of phone calls that you have to make every day knowing (regardless of the results) that will further your business and your success. **Athletic-related example**: following through in the daily process of studying your playbook, completing your workout, and making the right choices with your daily nutrition.

3. **Example of being in service of another**: random act of kindness for another (i.e., buying a cup of coffee anonymously for the next person in line at the coffee shop.)

Find what fires YOU up without exception and ignite that passion so that you routinely create *YOUR Prizefighter day*. Take your time. After watching the video, create your three focal points that are activity driven to give you the sense of accomplishment in creating a balanced life personally and professionally.

www.YOURPrizefighterDay.com

Before you know it, you will imperceptibly start to pull away from disempowering conversations, noting that even an "ordinary" day is a *Prizefighter Day* on your individual path to GREATNESS. Now, it is YOUR turn to build *YOUR Prizefighter Day*!

YOUR Legacy Statement

Once you complete YOUR Legacy Statement, you will have what you need to take action and feed your mind the positivity that lies within the statement to drive YOUR performance. At what point during the day would it make sense for you to read YOUR Legacy Statement?

We've seen business professionals and athletes drive significant success by reading and connecting to their Legacy Statement in the morning. In addition, they choose to read it when they feel like they have been knocked down during the day or when they face adversity or challenge. In addition, many find great fuel by once again revisiting their statement in the evening before they go to bed.

Staying deeply connected to the reasons WHY you want to continue to drive your performance is critical to achieving success on YOUR journey. YOUR Legacy Statement connects you to the reasons WHY you want to continue to make a difference. Take your time on this exercise and enjoy connecting to what drives YOU. Allow this to become the action step to fuel YOUR daily behaviors and drive peak performance in YOUR life.

YOUR Legacy Statement

This is the mental training tool that connects you to YOUR LEGACY. It's time to create YOUR blueprint for success in YOUR future. This is the tool that ties together all of YOUR mental training tools.

You will notice that YOUR Legacy Statement includes: YOUR Purpose Statement, YOUR "I AM" statements, YOUR 5-year vision and 1-year vision, YOUR Prizefighter Day, charity and service to others, quotes that FIRE YOU UP, the true measure of YOUR success, and, once again, reconnecting to YOUR "I AM" statements.

Purpose Statement: _____

_____

Who are YOU??? (YOUR 'I AM' Statements): _____

_____

5-year vision or 1-year vision: _____

_____

YOUR Prizefighter Day

1. Personal Activity _____

2. Business or Athletic Activity _____

3. Service Activity _____

Charity/Serving

Others _____

_____

Quotes that FIRE YOU UP!

1. _____

2. _____

What is the TRUE MEASURE of YOUR Success: _____

_____

Who are YOU??? (YOUR 'I AM' Statements): _____

_____

About the Author

Ben Newman
The Ben Newman Companies
www.BenNewman.net

Ben Newman is a bestselling author, international speaker, and highly regarded performance coach whose clients include Fortune 500 companies, business executives, high performing salespeople, and professional athletes in the NFL, MLB, and PGA, as well as the NCAA. Ben's most recent book, *Own YOUR Success*, was ranked by CEO READ as their #13 business book of 2012!

In addition, the Napoleon Hill Foundation & Nightingale-Conant selected Ben as a top thought leader and author in the world to help produce their latest audio book *Napoleon Hill's 17 Principles of Success*.

Known for his ability to inspire and motivate with actionable steps, Ben has presented to numerous FORTUNE 500 companies and other notable organizations, including the St. Louis Cardinals, the United States Army, the University of Iowa, Boston Medical Center, Australian Gold, NAIFA, AFA Singapore, MARS Snack Foods, the Minnesota Vikings, and more—helping their leaders grow and develop successful national sales teams for years. His corporate speaking events have included financial firms, religious groups, health care groups, charitable organizations, national sales organizations, sports teams, and communication companies.

Ben's authentic, powerful, and engaging presentations have become nationally recognized. Ben has shared the stage with Tony Dungy, Colin Powell, Brian Tracy, Ken Blanchard, Jon Gordon, Dr. Jason Selk, Floyd Little, Aeneas Williams, Tony LaRussa, Walt Jocketty, Tom Hegna, and other leaders and legends.

Ben lives in his hometown of St. Louis, Missouri, with the true measure of his success, his wife, Ami, and their children, J. Isaac and Kennedy Rose.

Resources available for YOU!

"YOUR success is not just about changing YOUR habits, it's about changing the way you think."

Ben Newman speaks to conventions and organizations all over the world. *The Ben Newman Companies*, a professional speaking and consulting company, conducts boot camps, seminars, and in-depth training in the areas of mental toughness, high-performance sales, teamwork, leadership, and relationship building.

Ben's customized speaking and coaching leaves audiences inspired, educated, AND empowered! Participants are able to uncover their true potential, readying them to create the life they are meant to fight for and enjoy. Emerging poised to take on THEIR relentless pursuit of greatness: Their *Prizefighter* day!

If you are interested in purpose-driven programs, based upon the principles of *Leave YOUR Legacy*, contact *The Ben Newman Companies*.

info@BenNewman.net

★ www.BenNewman.net ★

Other books by Ben Newman . . .

Own YOUR Success:
The Power to Choose Greatness and Make Every Day Victorious
—National bestseller and named by CEO Read as their
#13 Business Book of 2012!

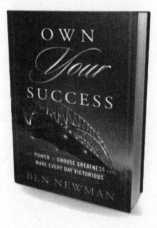

What if you could make each and every day victorious by focusing on daily activities rather than obsessing over results that you can't control? Based on author Ben Newman's popular program, *Own YOUR Success* gives you the power to make each day a triumph. The most successful people find great success when they focus on having a passion for the process. The key: make today victorious regardless of the obstacles that come your way. Figure out what fires YOU up without exception and ignite that passion so that you can routinely create your prizefighter day.

Own YOUR Success will lead you to uncover your true potential and create a life that belongs to YOU.

"*Own YOUR Success* is a wonderful book with a great message. Anyone will come away after reading this with a greater passion for life and a better sense of how to grow during the journey that we're all on."

—John Schlifske
CEO, Northwestern Mutual

Introduction to YOUR Mental Toughness Playbook

www.MentalToughnessPlaybook.com

Are you ready for the next level of YOUR success?

One of the first rules of sport psychology is for an athlete to perform at their highest level. They can't solely rely on their natural talents and abilities; they must understand the mental toughness side of what it takes to achieve peak performance.

I believe this is the same in anyone's life. This does not just apply to athletes, it applies to teachers, Fortune 500 executives, salespeople, professionals, those leading others in business and life. This concept applies to all individuals fighting to achieve peak performance in their lives.

This playbook and video series is about YOUR mental toughness and embracing the fact that your success is not just about changing your habits; it's about changing the way that you think. The most successful people are those who exemplify the importance of combining great habits and passion for the process with their ability to embrace adversity and challenge—to remain strong in driving their goals to completion.

In this program, we will explore six phases of YOUR Mental Toughness. The phases include Attaining Belief in Yourself, the Power to REFRAME, YOUR "I AM" statements, YOUR Prizefighter Day, YOUR Legacy Statement, and creating YOUR Environment for Greatness.

This is YOUR opportunity to drive more significant results in YOUR life by coupling the mental toughness side of what it takes to achieve peak performance with YOUR natural talents and abilities to serve others and make a difference in the world.

"The energy and enthusiasm for life in the room was off the charts during Ben's presentation. The LEGACY and mental toughness message that was delivered inspired all of us to strive for our potential as we prepare together for the next chapter of our Creighton Basketball program."

For Optimal Performance: YOUR Playbook course is to be used in conjunction with the online videos that pertain to each phase of the playbook. Let's GO DO GREAT THINGS!

—**Steve Merfeld,**
Creighton Men's Basketball
Assistant Head Coach

Fight the Good Fight: A Mother's Legacy Lives On

Fight the Good Fight provides inspiration for individuals who choose to embrace adversity in order to reach success. Over twenty years ago Ben Newman suffered the loss of his mother after years of watching her health deteriorate. After her tragic passing, his grandmother gave him an unexpected gift, in the form of a journal his mother left behind . . . A journey that is poignant, emotional, and sometimes heartbreaking, this is a story that you will remember forever in your soul.

"*Fight the Good Fight* is one of those quick reads that I had trouble putting down. The heart gets involved as Ben Newman exposes his own, with the tragedies that motivated him to help others. The idea of persistence and legacy are right on track with every successful athlete and businessman I know, and the insights in this book will hit the competitor in each of us, right between the eyes."

—**Mike Matheny**, Manager of the St. Louis Cardinals

Pocket Truths for Success: 365 Daily Principles to Become the Most Successful Person You Know

Pocket Truths for Success is your succinct guide to establishing priorities and achieving success in life. *Pocket Truths for Success* was written to be an inspiration for anyone facing the seemingly insurmountable challenges on the road to life's great successes. Personally and professionally, success is a difficult endeavor and possibly even harder to sustain once achieved. This book was written to address the two pivotal issues of achieving and sustaining success, in the complex ever-changing world we live in today. *Pocket Truths* delivers simple and powerful quotes for those ready to inspire and lead.

"*Pocket Truths* will inspire you to lead yourself, to lead others, and to make positive waves of change in the future. This book will concisely enable you to define your LEGACY!"

—**Jon Gordon**, *New York Times* Bestseller of *The Energy Bus*